SO-AHL-631

Tradition

BO SCHEMBECHLER'S MICHIGAN MEMORIES

by Bo Schembechler with Dan Ewald

Huron River Press
Ann Arbor, MI

Copyright © 2003 Clock Tower Press LLC

All rights reserved. No part of this book may be reproduced in any manner without the express written consent of the publisher, except in the case of brief excerpts in critical reviews and articles. All inquiries should be addressed to:

Huron River Press
3622 W.Liberty
Ann Arbor, MI 48103
www.huronriverpress.com

Huron River Press is an imprint of Clock Tower Press LLC.

Printed and bound in China
10 9 8 7 6 5 4 3 2 1

Library of Congress Cataloging-in-Publication Data

Schembechler, Bo.
Tradition : Bo Schembechler's Michigan memories / by Bo Schembechler
with Dan Ewald.
p. cm.
Originally published: Michigan memories. Chelsea, MI : Sleeping Bear
Press, 1998.
ISBN 1-932399-01-1
1. Schembechler, Bo. 2. Football coaches—United States—Biography.
3. Michigan Wolverines (Football team)—History. 4. University of
Michigan—Football—History. I. Ewald, Dan. II. Schembechler, Bo.
Michigan memories. III. Title.
GV939.S33A3 2003
796.332'092—dc21

2003004720

Inquiries regarding prints of Joseph Arcure's photographs contained in this book should be made at 800-761-3686 ext. 50, or at www.foto1.com.

The essence of Michigan Football lies not in the bodies of all those magnificent players who bravely take the field each Saturday in the fall. It lives proudly, rather, in the spirit of all the players, all the coaches, all the students, all the alumni and all the fans.

For all the men and women — past, present and future — who strive for excellence through honesty, integrity and hard work, this book belongs to you. That's the Michigan way.

— Bo Schembechler

ACKNOWLEDGMENTS

The authors wish to acknowledge all of the former University of Michigan Football players, coaches and staff who contributed so generously and unselfishly to the creation of this book. In addition, a special thanks is extended to Howard Wikel, Greg Kinney, Lloyd Carr, Don Lund, Don Dufek, Cathy Schembechler, Lynne Johnson, Mary Passink, the Bentley Historical Library and the University of Michigan Sports Media Relations Department.

FOREWORD

I t is, indeed, the fortunate person to be surrounded by men and women who exert a positive influence on the lives that they touch.

Rare, however, is the privilege of befriending an individual whose character transcends one generation after another, even years after his departure.

The measure of such people is extraordinarily high. Consequently, of course, their numbers are few. In my long political and professional career, I am honored to have had the good fortune to befriend a handful of such notables.

I am proud to include Coach Bo Schembechler in that number.

In a sport such as college football where success, too often, is measured simply by the number of wins and losses, Bo's accomplishments elevate him to the highest rung of coaching excellence.

The essence of Bo's legacy to the University of Michigan and beyond, however, transcends all the numbers and individual honors that fill all the record books. That's because it's impossible to attach numerical significance to the virtues of honesty, dignity and integrity that have served as the hallmarks in Bo's life, both on and off the field.

Having had the privilege of playing football and becoming a small part of the tradition at the University of Michigan, I remain acutely aware of the rewards derived from acquiring the discipline demanded from such an exacting sport. Valued lessons in life, discipline and an appreciation for the beauty of teamwork are sometimes better acquired on the field than in the classroom.

Few in the history of the game have imparted those invaluable humane and American virtues of honesty, dignity and integrity as consistently as has Bo. And because he has chosen to live his life in accordance to such high principle, his sphere of influence reaches far beyond the young men he led into football battle for the University of Michigan. With Bo, both on the field and off, there is only one way to live one's life – the right way.

The memories that Bo created for Michigan alumni and fans across the world are countless and priceless. Reliving some of those memories, along with some that were made before his arrival at Michigan, serves as a special source of pleasure and pride.

I thank Bo for sharing some of these special treasures with us. I salute him for refusing to compromise the principles he so steadfastly endears.

GERALD R. FORD
38th President
United States of America

Before Gerald Ford rose to the presidency; he distinguished himself as a Wolverine on the football field. On October 8, 1994 Ford's number 48 was officially retired during half time ceremonies. Only 5 Michigan numbers have been retired.

TABLE OF CONTENTS

"Tradition...what would you expect?"

INTRODUCTION

Bo Schembechler likes to think of himself as nothing more than "the ol' football coach." He didn't create the Michigan Football tradition. Fielding H. Yost beat him by about seven decades on that one.

Bo wasn't a football revolutionary. Fritz Crisler handled that with his inception of the two-platoon system and the famous winged helmets. Bo's preference was to "hit 'em clean." But also "hit 'em hard and often."

Bo's contribution to Michigan tradition touches another level. He's the godfather of the contemporary Michigan program. As former Athletic Director Don Canham simply states, "None of this would have happened if it hadn't been for Bo."

What Canham refers to is the most celebrated, successful, and revered college football tradition in the country.

Of course, Bo scoffs at the suggestion of his importance. That's exactly what "the ol' football coach" would do.

The numbers are staggering:

- More wins — 194 — than any coach in Michigan history.
- 13 Big Ten championships in a 21-year tenure.
- 17 post-season bowl games, including 10 Rose Bowls.
- 17 top-ten finishes in the final wire service polls.

As overwhelming as the numbers are, that's all they are — numbers. Bo is proud of them. But his strength is leading people and the spirit that he breathed into the proud Michigan tradition.

"Obviously he knows football," said former Michigan All-American Dan Dierdorf. "But he knows people even better. Bo has the ability to get a whole organization driving in the same direction. Not just the players, but all the coaches and assistants and secretaries and everyone that goes into making a successful organization."

Bo came to Michigan in 1969 when the program needed a little boost, at a time when college football was beginning to explode across national television networks.

The game was becoming big...very big. With Canham's genius for marketing and Bo's relentless drive for excellence, Michigan Football was propelled to the top of intercollegiate sports.

Now the game has grown into an industry of its own. Interest across the country borders on religious zeal. Revenues generated from those Saturday afternoons boggle the mind.

While the evolution is impressive, it's also extracted its price. The magnitude of the college football universe may have marked the end to such romantically colorful single-name figures such as Bo and Woody and The Bear.

Certainly the intensity of the Michigan-Ohio State rivalry increases each year. But what true Michigan fan doesn't miss that special tingle of the war within a war when Bo took on Woody and all those nasty boys from down south of the Michigan border?

For Bo, everything was simple. There was no hidden agenda. His focus was simple — make Michigan Men out of the boys he brought to the University and make the University proud of winning the right way.

Everything was done according to his three simple unbending principles of honesty, integrity, and hard work.

Bo was confident that his system would work. He also recognized the unique combination of academic and athletic excellence which only Michigan enjoys.

"That's the beauty about Bo," said Jim Brandstatter, one of his former players and a current radio and television analyst. "He never compromises his principles. I could see why a mother and father would feel good about sending their son to play for Bo and get an education at Michigan."

While Bo now is content that the program is in excellent hands under Coach Lloyd Carr, he should also take pride that the program is on course precisely because of his relentless pursuit of excellence.

No one coach or player or administrator is bigger than the program as a whole. As Bo himself always preached, "It's the team...the team...the team!"

Neither Bo nor anyone else would suggest that the Michigan Football tradition would have failed to thrive without him.

But his magnificent presence for those 21 very special years is still felt today.

In the following pages, "the ol' football coach" has assembled a scrapbook of Michigan memories. Many are personal ones that he had a hand in shaping. Others reflect the history of this staggering tradition.

Bo learned from this long tradition and then contributed chapters of his own before carefully passing on the program in excellent shape.

He now shares some memories that mean so much to so many people. There are glimpses of various personalities. There are pictures and stories of events that help to shape this singular tradition.

And there is assurance that this marvelous history will continue to be written in the Michigan way.

—Dan Ewald

THAT'S TRADITION!

Tradition is something you can't bottle.
You can't buy it at the corner store. But it is
there to sustain you when you need it most.
I've called upon it time and time again. And
so have countless other Michigan athletes
and coaches. There is nothing like it. I hope
it never dies.

— Fritz Crisler

t's been more than a half-century since Fritz Crisler defined the University of Michigan tradition. It's as alive today as it was back then. And it will still be alive a hundred years from now.

Here's exactly what Fritz was saying.

Tra-DI-tion is having one of the finest academic institutions in the country.

Tra-DI-tion is a football program that has put together more victories than any school in any division in history.

Tra-DI-tion is running that program with integrity and according to all the rules.

Tra-DI-tion is more than 110,000 people in a stadium over 75-years-old every football Saturday.

Tra-DI-tion is all the color and tailgating and spirit that comes together to make all those Saturdays in Ann Arbor like no other place in the whole United States of America.

That's Michigan Football.

THAT'S *tra-DI-tion!*

Tradition is a feeling. That's what it really is. It's a feeling that links the past to the present and builds a bridge to the future.

A lot of schools talk about tradition. But there is nothing like the tradition that lives at the University of Michigan.

We have it in our academic program. We have it throughout our campus.

And as sure as there are no greater helmets than those famous Michigan winged ones anywhere in the world, we have it in our football program.

First of all, when you talk about the University of Michigan, you're talking about as great a public

"Tra-DI-tion breeds in-TEN-si-ty."

institution as there is in America. It has attracted the brightest young people from all over the country and, nowadays, from all over the world.

Once all those people come to the university, they discover that part of that great tradition is Michigan Football.

It's those 110,000 people in that old red brick stadium. It's the great rivalries of Michigan and Ohio State...Michigan and Notre Dame...Michigan and Michigan State. It's reaching back to make one more great play when there's nothing left to give but determination alone.

THAT'S tradition!

After those young students graduate and move on to pursue careers all over the world, Michigan Football remains as a link to their university. During the whole week of every football season, they can hear about their team playing back at Michigan. And they know exactly what to expect.

They expect excellence. They expect winning according to all the rules. They can picture in their minds that whole spectacle going on back in Ann Arbor. It's their connection to the past.

The Michigan Football program must remain one of the finest in the country. With nationally ranked schools such as law and business and engineering and medicine and all the others, tradition challenges the Michigan Football program. It MUST always remain among the national elite.

We have built a football program here that will last. Anyone who has participated in it knows why it's so great. Anyone who has become attached to the program as a supporter or a fan shares in that tremendous pride. Michigan Football was built within the rules and it lives within the rules.

I don't believe you can have the tradition of Michigan Football without a long period of success. You don't build tradition on losing teams. No school in America has enjoyed the success of Michigan.

No other school can because no other school has won as many games as Michigan.

Tradition demands that we pass the torch from one generation to the next. For the coaches it's gone from Yost to Crisler to Schembechler to Carr. For the players it's gone from Heston to Oosterbaan to Harmon to Kramer to Dierdorf to Carter to Howard to Woodson.

Every coach, every player, every athletic director, every equipment manager, every trainer, every secretary that has worked in the football program shares in that tradition.

And so does every student, every former student and every fan who believes in a program that is more than a century old and still operates on the same principles of doing things the right way — with honesty and integrity!

Each game — from Fielding Yost's "point-a-minute" teams to the ones that are played on television screens across the nation each Saturday now — is a piece of that tradition that we call Michigan Football.

"They made it to the 1902 Rose Bowl, but today we'd NEVER take a picture with guys lying on the ground."

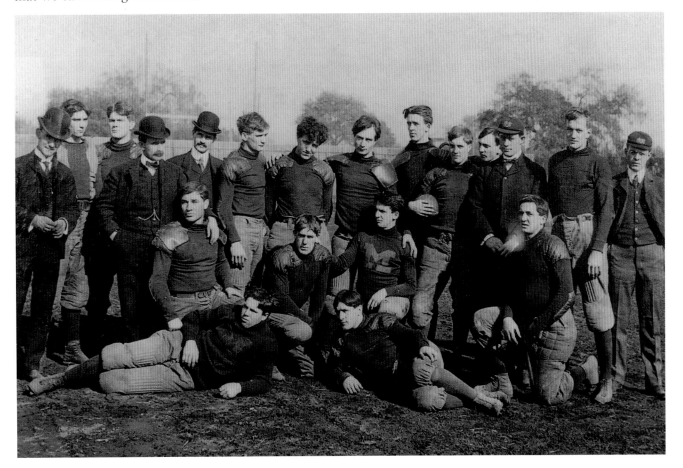

"They'd probably have their eyes open if they had worn face masks back then. Look at those empty seats. You won't see that at Michigan anymore."

All the touchdowns...all the interceptions...all the victories in the record books continually add to that tradition. Games that were won five, 10, 20, or more than 50 years ago still remain as alive today as the one played just last Saturday.

When you are able to relive all the plays and all the excitement of so many games from so long ago, that's the true measure of tradition. It just doesn't die.

The games will always be the heart of all those memories. But so many other elements are mixed into the magic of Michigan Football tradition.

There are the tailgate parties...the traffic jams to get to the games...all the Michigan flags...those airplanes flying over the stadium during the games...just the stadium itself.

Even today, every time I see that stadium I still can't imagine that Fielding Yost had the vision to construct such a masterpiece way back in 1927.

More people have watched college football in that stadium than any other facility in the world.

Just imagine — for every home game, year after year, more than 110,000 people cram into that park. For three hours during each game, that stadium holds more people than all but a handful of cities around the state.

"Great picture, but how would you like the seat of the guy who took it?"

"Now that's what I call punt coverage."

"Derrick Alexander was one of several great Michigan receivers, but he better get both hands on the ball or we're going to lose it!"

"When you tackle your own man like this, then you know there's a victory smile behind that face mask."

"When you fly over the stadium on a Michigan Football Saturday, I guess it's not a secret anymore."

"There was *never* a time running under that banner that I didn't jump up and touch it."

Each one of those people share in the Michigan Football tradition. Each one of them adds a little bit more to it.

And there isn't a bad seat in the house.

One of the most amazing parts of that stadium to me is the tunnel that leads to the field. As big as the stadium is, there's only one way onto that field. And there's only one way off.

You've got to go through that tunnel!

I'm not sure how a heavyweight champion feels when he walks up to the ring for a big fight. But it can't be any more electrifying than that walk through the tunnel to take the field for a Michigan football game.

It's dark in that tunnel when you come out of the locker room. The tunnel sort of grades down toward the field. As you get closer, it starts to get a little brighter.

Then all of a sudden, it hits you like a blinding light. When you finally line up to charge out on to that field in front of more than 110,000 screaming fans, there's absolutely no other feeling on God's earth that even comes close to matching it.

The letter winners from the other sports hold that "M" banner at the middle of the field. All of our guys jump up to touch it. That little leap is something all of our guys will cherish for the rest of their lives.

"Now do you think these guys are ready to play?"

I don't care how many times you've done it. A bolt of electricity shoots through your body every time you run out of that tunnel. Even if you're just watching, goose bumps jump up all over your body.

Sitting way up in the press box, I still feel it today. I still get chills today.

There's a special feeling for the Michigan Marching Band. That band has a tradition of its very own. And it's become as much a part of Michigan tradition as the maize and blue colors themselves.

They have their own building and their own marching area. People have endowed positions in the band just as they have in football.

The band members are not all music majors. Basically, they're kids who came out of their high school bands and wanted to become part of the tradition.

Competition to make the band is just like the competition in football. It's tough. Those kids who make it, though, appreciate what they had to go through. They carry that accomplishment for life.

"I love the band. And don't for one second think it isn't part of the whole tradition."

The tradition of that band goes back to Bill Revelli and George Cavender. Revelli was probably the greatest band leader of all time. People who played for him are conducting bands at other schools all over the country.

I love that band. And you better bet your boots it has an effect on the football team and all the players.

There were big games on the road when I insisted that our band go with us. We would never go to Columbus or South Bend or East Lansing without our band. I was not going to one of those schools and listen to their band without having ours there.

It was simple. We don't go without our band. That's how strongly I felt about it.

Their practice field isn't far from where the football team practices. The band would be running through their drills when we'd be running through ours.

When we were practicing for the opener or a big game, the band director would call me.

"You need me, Bo?" he'd ask.

"Yeah," I'd tell him.

"What time you want us?" he'd ask.

"Be ready at such and such a time," I'd tell him.

We'd be finishing up some drills. Then right at the time the director promised, we could hear the music as the band marched up to the practice field.

I'd call a halt to the practice. The band would surround the team and play "The Victors." All the players would sing the words. That's the greatest fight song ever written. It was a helluva scene.

THAT'S tradition!

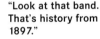

"Look at that band. That's history from 1897."

"I had Bill Revelli come to every fall meeting of the freshmen to teach them 'The Victors' — the greatest fight song in the history of intercollegiate athletics. He was the greatest band director in Michigan history. When I got here, he was the first man to visit my office. He said, 'I run this band like you run your football team.'"

"George Cavender took over where Revelli left off."

"That's the greatest band and the greatest fans waiting to greet the Michigan team. Look how neat those people look."

At other times practicing for big games, we'd play tapes of the band. Sometimes we'd play tapes of Bob Ufer calling some key plays in a big victory from years gone by.

You can't do all these things at other schools. You can't just go out and create tradition.

It has to develop decade after decade. And it must be shaped with honesty and integrity.

All these things are part of the Michigan Football tradition. All the parties, all the music, all the banners, all the old alumni coming back to games dressed in maize and blue. Everything plays a part in the most successful college football program in history.

Tradition is the feeling someone has for the university and everything that surrounds it.

Everybody runs into tough times. Sometimes a student is having a hard time in certain classes. Sometimes the football team is trailing by a touchdown with only a few minutes left to play.

That's when you reach back and tell yourself — "Hey, man...this is Michigan. I've got to do something about that right now."

If you play here or coach here, you automatically think in terms of not letting down all those people who started that tradition years and years ago.

There's a big shadow at Michigan. What kind of shadow is there at a losing school?

It's impossible to win every game. No team can. And there are valuable lessons to learn from every loss.

At Michigan, though, it's unforgivable to walk off that field with a drop of sweat left in your body.

That's the difference.

THAT'S tradition!

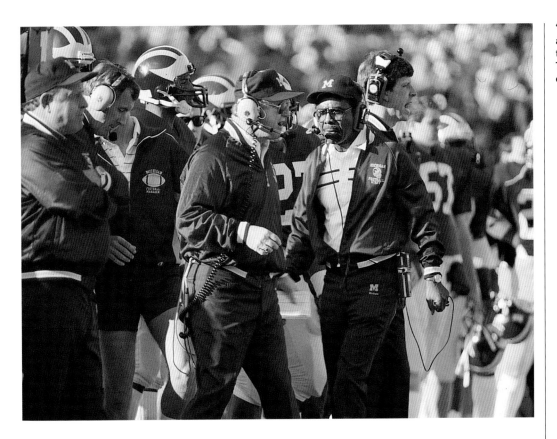

"A head coach is only as good as his assistants. I had the best. Terrell Burton was one of them."

"It takes intensity and alertness to create turnovers. Then you capitalize like Jarrett Irons did."

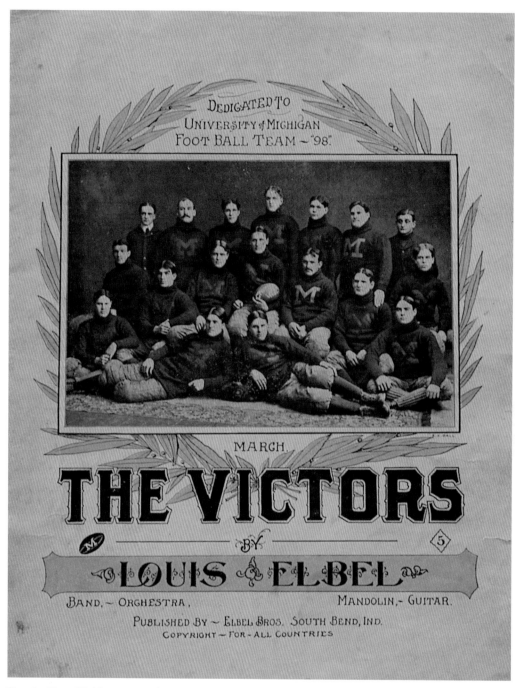

"Inspired by a Michigan upset victory over the powerful University of Chicago, coached by the legendary Amos Alonzo Stagg, 1898, Louis Elbel created *The Victors* walking from the field. Now more than a century old, it remains the most celebrated college fight song in America."

"The cheerleaders get the fans ready early."

THE HOLE TO GLORY

There's a hole in Michigan Stadium that plays a game with every player's mind each Saturday even before the real game begins.

It's midfield on the east side of the stadium. Like the ball that slowly descends each New Year's Eve in New York's Times Square, all eyes in the stadium are riveted to that hole as seconds tick down to kickoff.

It's the tunnel.

Well over 110,000 people for every game. But for players and coaches of both Michigan and their foes, there's only one way onto that magnificent field...and only one way off.

It's dark. It's dank. It's almost like some secret passageway carefully tucked away in time and used only for special — if not sacred — occasions.

It's far from aesthetically glamorous. Yet that drab concrete is richer with tradition than all the colorful murals and paintings of the world's most celebrated art galleries.

No player ever forgets his first trip down the tunnel. Even after several trips, the experience still causes shivers.

"The first time I did it I thought I was going to pee in my pants," said three-time All-American Ron Kramer. "There's no feeling like it. I can't put it into words."

As the team comes out of the locker room, players are jammed together like aspirin in a bottle. It's tight. And every person is one step from the edge.

It's shoulder pad to shoulder pad. Helmet to helmet. Every hulking player is sharing the same air. Even veteran seniors are as charged as raw freshmen.

"There is no greater feeling for player or coach than charging out of that tunnel in front of more than 110,000 people."

"It's tight in that tunnel...only one way in and one way out!"

"When I was in school, freshmen weren't eligible," said All-American Dan Dierdorf who is a member of the National Football League Hall of Fame. "So I'd go into the stadium when it was empty and just dream about how it must feel to charge out of that tunnel.

"There's no way to describe just how big that stadium is when you come out. There's more than a hundred-thousand people and you can't see a single one. It's like a snapshot. One minute you're in darkness and the next you're in the middle of the whole deal. It takes your breath away."

Once that signal is made, all the players, coaches, and team personnel charge from that tunnel and leap up to touch the "M" banner which varsity athletes from other sports hold in the middle of the field.

It's emotional. It also can be intimidating.

"Some visiting coaches have a difficult time just preparing their teams to take the field here," said Terrell Burton, one of Bo's long-time assistants.

"It's mind-boggling. When you come out of that tunnel, all you see is this sea of people. Opposing teams get the feeling that not only do they have to play our team but also all these people."

For part of his career, Burton worked games from the press box.

"I'd watch how our team charged out of that tunnel," he said. "You could get a feeling of how they were going to play just by the way they took the field."

The tunnel also is a valuable recruiting tool.

"Where else in the country can you take a young man into a stadium like this and then walk him down that tunnel which creates a feeling like nothing else in the world?" Burton asks.

Nowhere. It's part of the tradition. One way in...and one way out.

SPIRIT FROM THE SIDELINES

Millions of people have fallen for Michigan Football. No one, perhaps, has taken more tumbles though than Newt Loken.

The former Michigan gymnastics coach tumbled, jumped, screamed and hollered while weaving the cheerleading squad into the fabric of Michigan Football tradition.

"We tried to lead cheers for the team, not just perform," explains the sprightly Loken who was an active part of the tradition from 1947 through 1983.

"All those Michigan fans are packed into that stadium and their emotions want to come out. We tried to follow the crowd, not neces-sarily lead them. They're ready to respond. We were doing what all of them felt inside."

From Crisler to Oosterbaan to Elliott to Bo, Loken and his crew pumped plenty of life into the students, alumni, faculty and a variety of Wolverine loyalists.

"I loved those old Friday night pep rallies," Loken recalls. They were held mostly in front of the graduate library and sometimes where Ferry Field used to stand.

"I had the pleasure of introducing Bo at some of them. He was one of the most inspiring speakers I've ever heard. He could really turn a crowd on."

Before anyone took the microphone at the

"It must have been a Friday in front of the Michigan Union."

Newt Loken and the cheerleaders—part of the romance of Michigan Football.

rallies, the speaker was told to roll up his pant legs.

"Roll 'em up...roll 'em up," the crowd would yell. "It was just an old tradition to spice things up."

Loken's squads started the tradition of doing a backflip off the rail of the wall that surrounds the stadium for each point Michigan scored. By the time the Wolverines had finished running up some scores, the squad got a little dizzy.

When Loken arrived at Michigan after World War II, the cheerleading squad consisted of eight to ten members of the men's gymnastics team. It wasn't until early in the '70s that the team welcomed coeds. Today the team consists of nine men and nine women. All have at least some gymnastics experience.

Loken still attends all the Michigan home games and particularly enjoys Homecoming.

"About 75 old-timers always come back to join the current team and the band on the field," he said. "It brings back a lot of warm memories."

The game, of course, is always the focal point of any Michigan Football Saturday. But the extras like the cheerleaders and band and tailgaters comprise the total Michigan experience.

"All those things bring life to the experience," Loken says. "They're all part of the romance."

The last time Michigan played before a home crowd of less than 100,000 was October 25, 1975, when a game with Indiana drew 93,857.

And it's not likely to happen again for a long, long time.

"Now the teams are so good and the population has increased so dramatically they're probably going to be sold out till the end of time," Canham said.

It's the game. It's the spectacle. It's the treasure of the Michigan Football tradition.

"If there's any item that doesn't have an 'M' on it today, there'll be one on it tomorrow."

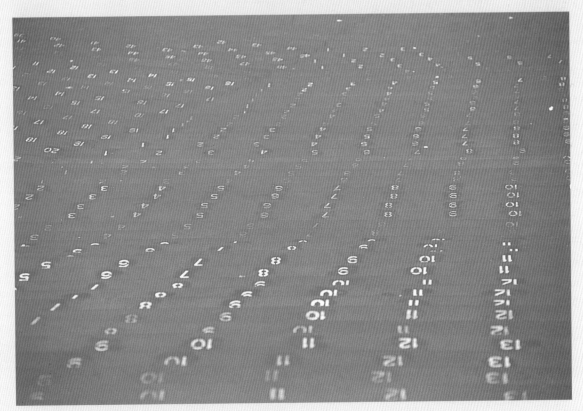

"There used to be empty seats. Try finding some today."

PLAYING TO A FULL HOUSE

It's "The Big House."

Size alone, however, incompletely paints all the romance, charm, and color of Michigan Stadium. The immensity of The Big House is complemented by its grandfatherly maturity.

Now in its eighth decade of existence, Michigan Stadium remains as vibrant today as the day it opened its gates on October 1, 1927.

No building, stadium, or any type of edifice is expected to retain that type of vitality.

Of course, Michigan Stadium is unlike any other facility in intercollegiate sports.

• There is the mystique of football's largest facility.

• There is the 100,000-person record for every home game since November 8, 1975.

• There are those inviting rustic red bricks and black iron fencing that captures a special collegiate charm from so many years ago.

• There is that singular thrill of walking into the stadium and being able to look down

"I love it. For fans and players, it's the best stadium in the country."

at one of the most meticulously manicured playing fields in America.

• There is Champions Plaza.

• There are rows of permanently inset inscribed bricks decorating the plaza from Michigan supporters.

• And there are countless millions of memories never to be forgotten from all the Michigan men and women who have proudly contributed to the Michigan Football tradition.

And it all goes back to Fielding H. Yost.

"A lot of people thought he was crazy at the time," said the late lifelong Ann Arbor resident Kip Taylor, who scored the first touchdown in The Big House.

"I think it was Mr. Yost who got the last laugh."

Everyone now shares a proud smile as the stadium stands as a monument to the most successful football program in intercollegiate history.

"When I took recruits into the tunnel, I used to tell them that if they thought football is a religion...you are now entering the greatest cathedral in the United States," said Jerry Hanlon, who served as an assistant

throughout Bo's tenure. "It's hard to explain, but this stadium is unique. There are a lot of other pretty ones, but none have the aura or tradition that this one has."

Before the stadium opened, Michigan played its home games at Ferry Field, which was located where the Michigan outdoor track now stands. Prior to that, Michigan played at Regents Field.

Yost's vision for the finest athletic complex

in the country eventually persuaded the University to spend $240,000 on the land where the stadium now stands.

"There was nothing but a strawberry patch and a barn sitting on top of an underground spring," Taylor recalled. "I remember it well. Only Mr. Yost could have envisioned what it would become."

Yost imagined a day when Michigan football would demand seating for 130,000 people.

"He was so far ahead of his time," said Don Lund, who won nine varsity letters and later served as Associate Athletic Director. "He had the stadium built with double footings so it can easily be expanded. He knew people would get bigger so he had entrances built wider."

Yost didn't stop with the stadium. He built the nation's first athletic field house and intramural building. He also built one of the finest golf courses in the Midwest.

"When they dug dirt for the stadium, there

"The Eagle was dedicated in 1948 to the memory of the men and women of the University of Michigan who gave their lives for our country in World War II."

was this big hole in the ground," Taylor said. "There were springs, so there was water all over the place. Mr. Yost said, `That's O.K... we'll just pipe it across the street and build a golf course.'"

And what a course it turned out to be! Yost hired legendary Alister MacKenzie to design it. Two of MacKenzie's other designs are the Augusta National and Cypress Point on the Monterey Peninsula.

But it's Michigan Stadium that remains as the "cathedral" for what all of college football represents.

With a seating capacity of 107,701, it's the largest football facility in intercollegiate athletics.

Size alone, however, comprises only part of the spirit of the Michigan Football tradition.

"How about this Homecoming?"

"Here's the big hole that got it all started."

"Early on the stadium was almost flush with the level of the ground."

"Any time of day or any time of year, it's a piece of art."

A FIELD FOR CHAMPIONS

It's been called the most prominent two acres of field anywhere in America.

It's the Broadway of college football...the ultimate stage where tradition begins.

That 100-yard tract sitting in the middle of the Big House is precious, priceless and dripping with myth and legend now closing in on the latter part of a century.

Bo's teams played their games on Tartan Turf and All Pro Turf before the university switched to natural grass after Gary Moeller's first season in 1990.

After a dozen years of natural grass, a state-of-the-art artificial surface called "Field Turf" now is the focal point of the most celebrated stadium in college sports.

"Michigan Stadium is the most revered football stadium in America," explained Executive Associate Athletic Director Mike Stevenson, who was responsible for the installation of the new surface in the spring of 2003.

"We want the very best facility and surface we can provide for our student-athletes. This is the finest surface on which elite athletes can perform to their highest level. It ensures that games will be determined by athletes and not the field."

The game has evolved into a battle of speed and skill. This innovative surface allows the nation's elite players to utilize their talents without concern for the surface.

"Field Turf" is the closest thing to natural grass as humanly possible," Stevenson said. "It looks like grass and even feels like grass. The beautiful part is that it's stable from end zone to end zone, sideline to sideline. It provides a fast track and remains consistent regardless of weather conditions from late summer through November."

And there are no more rug burns as from old synthetic surfaces.

"Players love it," Stevenson said. "It allows them to utilize their skills to the maximum. It will become a valuable recruiting tool."

"Field Turf" is comprised of 70% crumb rubber (attained from old tires and shoes) which is frozen, crystallized and then broken into tiny pieces before being combined with sand. The rubber produces a cushion effect and the sand provides stability. Grass fibers of $2\frac{1}{2}$ to $2\frac{3}{4}$ inches provide an aesthetically pleasing appearance. Because of its superb drainage capability, a minimal crown is necessary which guarantees consistency to the whole field.

This is the surface used at the Detroit Lions' Ford Field and also at Oosterbaan Fieldhouse, Michigan's indoor practice facility. The Universities of Oregon and Washington and the NFL's Seattle Seahawks, all located in heavy rain areas, have enjoyed the benefits of the modern marvel.

Many major universities – and even high school programs – have converted to "Field Turf." Michigan spent $620,000 for the project that includes the new surface, renovation of the border surrounding the field, new rubber matting in the tunnel and an upgrade to the drainage system.

It's the Big House. It must be the best.

"Even when he was President, Gerald Ford loved coming to our practices. He ate at our training table. He liked to get in the huddle. The problem was that there were always Secret Service agents around him. My players asked what they should do if the agents got in the way of a play. I told my men to run them over."

A good number of physicians, lawyers, educators, and international business leaders also matured through the program.

None, however, left his mark on world history as profoundly as a 1935 graduate who went on to become the 38th President of the United States of America.

Gerald Ford earned that distinction in 1974 after serving a short time as Vice President and several years as a leading Congressman in the House of Representatives.

He's the only former President to have played on two national championship teams (1932-1933). In 1934 he was named Michigan's Most Valuable Player as a center.

"Even before I went to Michigan, I felt there was something very special and wonderful about its tradition," he said. "It's vibrant, stimulating, and has a certain wholesomeness. I've retained that feeling throughout my life and remain very loyal to the program. I follow all of Michigan's fortunes quite closely. It's impossible not to have been imbued by that long tradition of Yost and Crisler and Schembechler."

President Ford played under Coach Harry Kipke. During Mr. Ford's first two varsity seasons, the Wolverines posted a 15-0-1 record.

In his senior year, they fell to 1-7. Of course, no other 1-7 team in history had a center who went on to become President of the United States.

"Some of the lessons I learned from competition on the football field were as valuable as any that I learned in the classroom," he said. "The concept of teamwork has always been particularly impressed upon all Michigan teams."

As with all former Michigan football players, President Ford fondly recalls how the University's present was always touched by its proud past.

"When I played, Fielding Yost was the Athletic Director," he said. "He was truly a living legend. I remember him coming around to our practices. That hat of his was always half-cocked on his head. He never smoked it, but he always was chewing on a cigar."

President Ford has been a frequent visitor to his school's games and even some practices.

During halftime of the Michigan State game, on October 8, 1994, President Ford's No. 48 was retired. It is one of just five numbers to have been retired by the University.

No. 48 from the Class of 1935 not only left his mark on Michigan tradition, but also on American history.

KEEPER OF HELMETS AND SECRETS GALORE

Jon Falk is like one of those hundreds of helmets for which he's responsible. It's easy to take a helmet for granted. But no one is fool enough to play a game without one.

Falk is the Michigan Football Equipment Manager. He's responsible for all the equipment and facilities. With about 110 players during the heat of a season, the job can be unnerving.

For instance, Falk oversees the distribution and upkeep of nearly 2,000 pairs of shoes and 300 of those celebrated winged-tip helmets. Each day during the season, he and his crew wash about 800 pounds of uniforms, towels, and miscellaneous equipment.

In any collegiate or professional sport, few are privy to all the little secrets of a program as is the equipment manager. It's the nature of the position. They arrive long before any of the players and still are there after they've gone. Any tricky problem can usually be solved by the equipment manager.

Falk has held the Michigan head job since 1974. There's an unwritten rule in sports that certain stories never leave the locker room. Some experiences, though, make the long hours all worthwhile.

There was that frigid January evening in 1985 when, driving down I-94, Falk spotted a frozen figure hitchhiking on the shoulder. He thought the hat on the figure looked curiously like that of Bo's. The stalled car also resembled that of the coach.

"Jon Falk is one of the best equipment managers in the country. He does a great job with the equipment and a great job with the players...as long as he doesn't try to coach too much."

Falk pulled over and sure enough...there was Bo.

"He was caked with ice," Falk recalled. "His hands were, literally, shaking."

"Where are you going?" Bo asked his equipment manager.

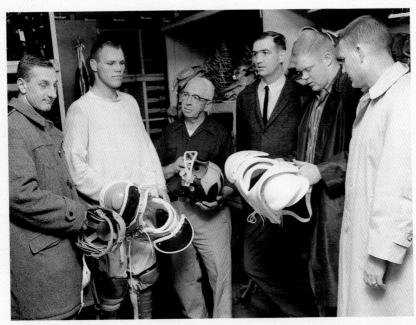

"Henry Hatch (third from left) was a legend at Michigan. Bill Freehan (second from left) could have been a good one here. But he did all right with the Detroit Tigers."

"Well, Bo, I sort of had plans," Falk answered.

"Well, you've got new plans now," Bo said as Falk drove him home.

After thawing a little, Bo told Falk that three state police cars had passed while he was thumbing a ride.

"Well, Bo, we did finish 6-6 last year," Falk cracked.

Bo not only respected Falk's professionalism over the years, but enjoyed having him around.

After a press conference at which Bo announced he was stepping down as coach, he went to his usual locker in the coaches' room to prepare for a personal workout. It's always been Falk's policy to clear a locker as soon as someone leaves.

When Bo got to his, it was cleaner than Old Mother Hubbard's cupboard.

"Falk," Bo shouted. "You've got me cleaned out already?"

"They come and they go, Hobbs," Falk said, borrowing a line from *The Natural*.

"They come and they go."

Falk's position provides a unique perspective on the coaches he serves. Although he concedes their personalities are different, Falk sees striking similarities between Bo and Lloyd Carr.

"I told Lloyd there's a lot of Bo in him," Falk said. "Bo was tough and no nonsense. There was nothing more important to Bo than his players. He demanded the best for all of them, even those who didn't play.

"Bo always recruited the kids who had character along with talent. It's the same thing Lloyd does. Those are the kind of kids who can be coached and turned into champions. Those are the kids that Michigan wants."

"Look at those old-timers turn out those football shoes. We had them long before Nike came along."

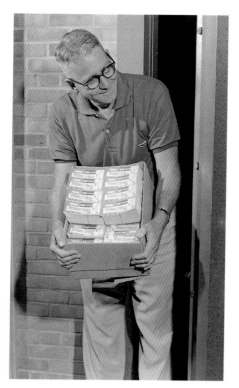

"Ticket Director Don Weir used to count them by hand."

"I hope that guy gets lucky."

"This guy's got to be crazy to sell those two."

"Even in the old days, someone always needed a pair."

"You couldn't speak at a pep rally if you didn't 'roll them up.'"

"Now that's getting down and dirty for the team in the old Mud Bowl."

"That's the train station back in the '30s (now the Gandy Dancer) and they're waiting for the Michigan team."

"Those people are waiting for the 1997 National Champions."

"I love his enthusiasm, but I hope his mother doesn't recognize him."

"Roads were a little more narrow back then, but they all led to a good old-fashioned football game."

"They're all coming to the Big House. That's the kind of traffic jam I like to see."

"That old golf course has seen a lot of different car models over the years."

"A young entrepreneur."

"By car, by rail, by bus...everyone wants to get to a Michigan game."

"The early days of crowd control."

HOME SWEET HOME

Before the Big House, there was football at Michigan. In fact, the Wolverines had a few homes before Michigan Stadium opened in 1927.

From 1883 through 1892, Michigan played its home games at fields in Ann Arbor and Detroit. In 1893, "The Athletic Field," later known as Regents Field, opened with seating for 400 fans. With the erection of temporary bleachers to accommodate up to 17,000, the Wolverines compiled an impressive 87-2-3 record in all games at Regents Field.

In 1902, the name of the complex was changed to Ferry Field in honor of Detroit native Dexter Ferry who donated 21 acres. In 1906, the Wolverines moved to a new site on that donated land, located where the Michigan outdoor track now stands.

A maze of hash marks speckled Ferry Field. From 1903 until 1912, a team had three downs to advance the ball five yards toward the goal (increased to 10 yards in 1906). The first player to receive the ball had to cross the scrimmage line at least five yards left or right of where the ball was put into play.

In 1914, concrete stands increased the capacity of Ferry Field to 25,000 and in 1921, expansion stretched it to 40,000.

Then along came the Big House.

In 1925, the land where Michigan Stadium stands was purchased for $240,000. The Michigan Board of Athletics offered bonds at a price of $500 each to pay for stadium construction.

At a cost of $950,000, the stadium opened in 1927 with a structure housing 70 rows designed for 72,000 fans. With the addition of wooden bleachers, it hosted 84,401. Increased capacity continues right to the present as the Big House reigns as king of all football.

"They had aerial shots even back then."

"Look at those hats on the boys cramming into Ferry Field."

"That's Ferry Field at the 1904 University of Chicago game. Have you ever seen so many hash marks in your life?"

AND IF YOU'RE STRONG ENOUGH TO STAY...

Those Who Stay Will Be Champions.

— **Bo Schembechler**

 o one involved with Michigan Football will ever forget spring practice my first year here in 1969.

We inherited a good team. They had gone 8-2 the year before.

But one of those losses was brutal. They were humiliated at Ohio State, 50-14. There's no question that, at that time, Ohio State had the best team in college football...arguably the best ever.

At Michigan, we just couldn't let that happen.

The Michigan team had a lot of talent. We made it our goal to make that team TOUGH.

We had to take that talent and make it MEAN. I wanted them so mean that they'd scare themselves when they bumped into each other.

NO-body was going to out-hit us. NO-body was going to out-hustle us. If we got beat, it was because the other team on that day played a little better than we did. No team, though, was ever going to out-work us. NO TEAM!

That spring practice was hell for all those players. I mean a true living hell. We had a lot of attrition.

That's when I put up a sign that hung over my office over the years — "Those Who Stay Will Be Champions."

The sign cost $300. At the time, that was a lot of money for a sign. Don Canham really got upset. It was a beautiful sign, though.

When Canham got the bill he called me immediately.

"Schembechler...what the hell is this?" he screamed.

"We need that sign," I said. "Don't worry."

We wanted commitment. We told those players that if they made a commitment, they'd become champions.

All those young men who stayed did become champions. And so did the ones after them. And the ones

59

THOSE WHO STAY WILL BE CHAMPIONS

after them.

That's what Michigan Football is about — CHAMPIONS.

Players make championships. Not just players who have talent. Talent alone is a good start.

Champions, though, are carved out of character. Without character, talent can be beaten.

Give me a good team with players full of character and I'll take them over a great team with no character.

Michigan football builds character. In the long run, character always wins.

We hear about all the All-American players. They get the headlines. They deserve them. Their names will live forever. Guys like...Mandich...Dierdorf...McKenzie...Carter...Leach...Howard...Woodson. Over the years, we've been blessed with several at Michigan.

But I'm just as proud of every young man who put on that Michigan uniform and stuck it out for four years even when he didn't have a chance to play a game.

A lot of guys come here thinking they're going to have a great playing career. All of a sudden they discover there are two or three players at their position who are just a little bit bigger and a little bit quicker.

But these guys show up for practice day after day. They suit up for the demonstration team. They get bruised and bloodied and beat up. Their only chance to play is in some lopsided game.

They don't complain, though. They just grind it out.

When they graduate, people think they didn't have such a good career.

I think they had a GREAT career. They showed character. Michigan Football is all about character. We could not have won without each and every one of them.

That's why I changed the rules for winning a Michigan letter. It used to be based on the amount of time played.

"That's the 1902 Rose Bowl. And Michigan was there!"

Weeks. Shorts, Snow, Heston, Herrnstein

TACKLE-BACK-RIGHT PLAY.

For me, if a young man came out to practice every day for four years...if he hustled...if he sweat...if he bled...then he earned a letter the same as any player who started every game.

Most of these guys go out and make something of their lives. They understand the most important lesson Michigan Football can teach — the only way to individual success is through the success of a team.

They don't learn that from a book. They don't learn that in a classroom. They learn it from Michigan Football.

And they carry that lesson for the rest of their lives.

Jimmy Hackett was one of those guys. He was our demonstration team center in 1976. Today he's the president of the Steelcase Company. That's the largest manufacturer of office furniture in the world.

Not so long ago, I told Jimmy how proud I am of him.

"Coach," he told me, "I run this company exactly the way you ran Michigan

"Look at Charles Woodson slip through all those defenders."

"That's sweat. That's Michigan. That's Derrick Walker (top) and John Kolesar (bottom)."

"Chris Howard did everything for that one extra yard."

"Even on the sidelines, everybody stays in the game."

Football. Any man who works here — all 12,000 — who wants an appointment with me gets it."

Hackett was our third-team center. And when he wanted to talk to me, all he had to do was come to the office. Or pick up the phone. He meant just as much to me as the starting quarterback. Jimmy remembers that.

"You can't see all those guys," I said.

"Coach, I can work everybody in," he said. "It doesn't take up my whole day. And I'll tell you one thing — after talking to the guys in the plant, I know more about what's going on than I do from all the guys who surround me in the executive suite."

I had a rule. I never wanted to be interrupted during a meeting — unless a player wanted to talk to me.

I don't care if I was talking to the president of the university or if I was in the middle of a television interview. And it didn't matter if the player was an All-American senior or the 125th man on the team.

If that young man wanted to talk to me, then he got the time. He might have been in some kind of trouble. It might have taken a lot of courage to tell me something. If I tell him to come back in a couple of hours, he might never come back.

That's just not RIGHT.

"Jimmy Hackett didn't get to play much, but he made a great contribution to our success."

That's the way you build a team. Every one of those 125 players is part of that team.

I never lied to them and I never expected them to lie to me. That's all part of building a team with integrity. That's all part of Michigan Football.

One of the greatest success stories of my career involved a player who had no business even coming out for the team.

This guy had no chance to play. NONE!

He wound up playing middle guard on our undefeated 1973 team. Now he's gone on to become an executive at the Ford Motor Company.

In the summer of 1970, I was sitting in my office when this incoming freshman asked my secretary if he could see me.

"Coach Schembechler, my name is Don Warner," he said. "I've been admitted to the school of Engineering. I'm here for orientation and I want to come out for football."

He was about 5-foot-10, 175-pounds and a cocky little son of a gun. I figured he had to be a halfback who still needed to put on a few pounds to keep from becoming a pancake.

"You do?" I said. "What position do you play?"

"Offensive guard," he shot back.

Now I'm getting a little amused.

"Where did you go to school?" I asked him.

He said he had graduated from Dearborn Divine Child.

I had visited Divine Child. They had four real fine players the previous year who were recruited to Division I schools.

"I've seen Divine Child," I told him. "I don't remember you.

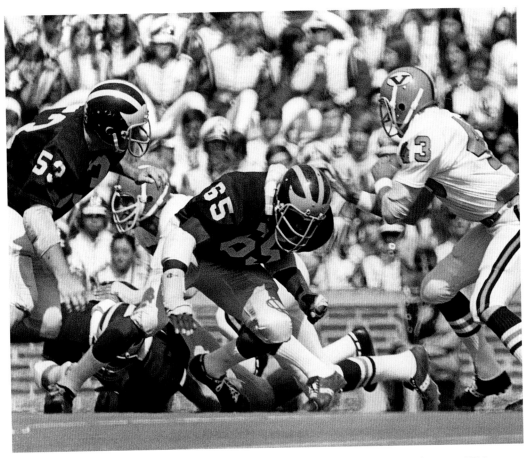

"Do not mess with
No. 65. THAT'S Mr.
McKenzie."

And besides, do you know who plays offensive guard here at Michigan? We've got Reggie McKenzie at 6-5 and 265 pounds. We've got Tom Coyle at 6-3 and 260 pounds. Now where in the heck are you going to fit in?"

He looked me in the eye. He never flinched.

"O.K.," he said. "If I'm too small to play offensive guard, I'll play middle guard on defense."

Now he's got me going.

"If you play middle guard, McKenzie and Coyle are the guys who are going to knock you from one side of the field to the other," I said. "I'm not going to let you come out. You're wasting our time. More important than that, you're going to get killed."

He still didn't flinch. He reminded me that I had spoken at the Divine Child football banquet.

"You told us that if we make up our minds to do something, never let anyone talk us out of it," he said.

Now he's really got me going.

"Why you little smart aleck kid," I said. "I'll tell you what I'm going to do. I'm going to let you come out. But as soon as you find out that you're not big enough to handle it, you quit. And I'll never look at you as a quitter because you showed me something just to go out there in the first place."

He thanked me and promised he'd never quit.

"If Reggie didn't get
you, then Tom Coyle
(60) did."

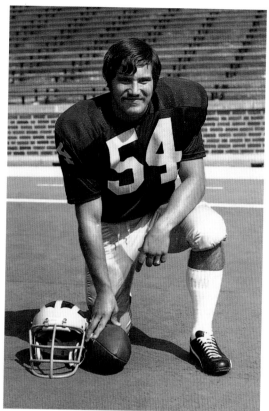

"Donnie (54) was a little short on size but awfully big on heart."

That whole first year he came out to practice every day. We put him on the demonstration team for the last four or five plays of the day and those big guys knocked him all the way to Ypsilanti.

At the end of the season, I called Donnie into my office just like I talked to every player.

"I don't know how you did it, but you stayed out there the whole season and I admire you," I told him. "But you realize now that you're too small to play here."

Just like he did at the beginning of the season, he never flinched.

"No, Coach," he said. "I know what I have to do. I'm going to lift weights, get bigger, and be out here next spring."

He came back the next year...and the next. He was playing on the demonstration team his junior year and actually started to stop some of the plays we were practicing.

"If we can't block Warner, how in the heck are we going to win Saturday?" I asked my coaches.

Finally in spring practice before his senior year, he's still out there. He was about 195 pounds by then and quick as a cat. Our first two middle guards had graduated. I told our coaches to put Warner No. 1 on the depth chart. I figured one of our young players would beat him out in the fall.

Well, let me tell you something. He came out that next fall and made up his mind that NOBODY was going to beat him out.

He had a mind like a computer. He studied the moves of every player. He knew when they were going to move to their left or move to their right. He knew when a guard was going to block for a run or drop back to protect on a pass.

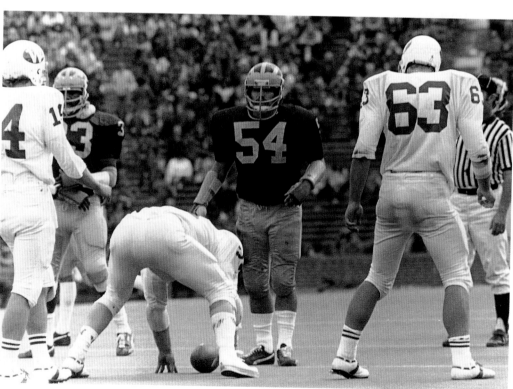

"Dennis Franklin's winning percentage at Michigan was greater than any quarterback in history and he never got a chance to play in a Rose Bowl. We fixed that rule!"

He started every game that 1973 season and we went into the Ohio State showdown undefeated. During the week between classes, Warner was in the projection room all the time. He studied every film of the season on Ohio State.

On the Thursday before the game, I walked out of my office to use the men's room and happened to run into Warner.

"I want you to know, Coach, I studied every film," he told me. "I got their center down cold. He's the best one we've played. Don't worry, though. I know when he's going left and I know when he's going right. I know the splits between the guards. I know what I have to do.

"No one man can block me. When they put two men on me, you get the linebacker to scrape into the hole. If we stop their run, we are going to win because they can't beat us passing."

I just stood there and listened to him talk.

"I'm glad I ran into you," I said.

At the end of the first half that Saturday, we were down, 10-0. Our whole defense was madder than a wild bull. They all were shouting — "Just score 11 and we'll win. They'll never score another point!"

Sure enough, in the second half we scored 10 and finished in a tie.

In the fourth quarter in the series before our quarterback, Dennis Franklin, went down with a broken collarbone, Warner went down with a knee injury. They had to help him off the field.

"Now it's Dr. Tom Slade."

For four years I thought he was going to get killed. And this was the first time he ever got hurt enough to come out of a game or even a practice.

Dr. O'Connor drove both players to the hospital. Warner's career was finished. He was going to have surgery the next day. Warner was sitting in the back of the car with his leg stretched out across the seat.

"Denny, don't worry," he said to Franklin. "When we go to the Rose Bowl, Larry Cipa will do a great job substituting for you. But who in the hell are we going to get to play middle guard?"

That was Donnie Warner. He was a kid who had no business playing here and wound up starting for an undefeated team...on sheer guts and determination.

THAT is Michigan Football!

Tom Slade was another kid who never knew how to quit. In 1971 he was our starting quarterback. The next year he got beat out by Dennis Franklin.

I told Slade that he would be holding on kicks and playing back-up. He never gave up. He came out and worked hard every day as if he was still starting. He learned a lot from his experience in Michigan Football. Today he's my dentist.

This is all part of the Michigan Football tradition. It goes all the way back to Yost to Crisler to Carr today.

That's why every time Michigan Football takes a bad rap, I take it personally. All the coaches, all the players, and all the fans do.

The Michigan Football tradition is filled with character. It's the heart of the program. And character isn't restricted only to All-Americans. Just ask Donnie Warner.

THIS MAGIC MOMENT

Kip Taylor was always proud to be a treasured piece of trivia in the fabled history of Michigan Football.

The year was 1927. Babe Ruth dominated the American sports scene by blasting 60 home runs for the New York Yankees. In Ann Arbor, Fielding H. Yost opened Michigan Stadium – now almost eight decades later, still the shrine of major college football.

The date was October 1st and Michigan crushed Ohio Wesleyan, 33-0.

Taylor was a sophomore end for the Wolverines. In his first varsity game before 17,877 persons, Taylor scored the first touchdown in Michigan Stadium history.

It was one of those magic moments in time.

Up to the day he died in 2002, still in his beloved Ann Arbor, Taylor's eyes sparkled whenever he recalled his moment of glory.

"Bennie Oosterbaan was the other end," Taylor never minded retelling the tale. "He was a three-time All-American so they were covering him pretty tight. I went back to the huddle and said that I was wide open. I went out and got open again. Louis Gilbert hit me with a 28-yard pass and we were on the board. The rest is history."

Even in his later years, once in a while Taylor found his way over to Michigan Stadium. He watched almost all the games on television and got as nervous as he did when he performed on that field.

"I sit there and bite my nails," he explained. "There's nothing in college sports that matches Michigan Football. Who ever thought it would get to be 110,000 people

every Saturday with people coming to town the night before? I love it."

Taylor said he "still got chills" when he thought about his magic moment in history so many years ago. So many other great ones have followed. This one, however, is forever locked in time.

CALLING A CHOSEN FEW

"You've got to recruit them and you've got to coach them. Rick Leach was a leader for Michigan for four straight years."

Over the years, college football recruiting has undergone more face-lifts than the Gabor sisters.

In spite of myriad changes, there remains at least one constant.

Recruiters for the University of Michigan are always welcomed through the front door.

"When I recruited for Michigan, I never went into a house through the back door," said long-time Bo assistant Jerry Hanlon.

"When you recruit for Michigan, you not only represent an outstanding football program, but also a university which the parents and high school teachers all want their kids to be associated with."

Although the annual recruiting war for the nation's finest high school prospects has bitterly intensified, Michigan's arsenal of weapons could fill a whole section of "The Big House." Some include:

• Tradition — the opportunity to play for a team that is nationally ranked annually.

• Coaching — one of the most dedicated all-around coaching staffs in the country.

• Stadium — not only the largest, but also the most prestigious stadium in college football.

• Facilities — with Schembechler Hall and the indoor practice field, the model for inter-collegiate excellence.

• Education — the University tops most lists of public institutions in the United States.

"There are a lot of fine schools and a lot of very good football programs around the country," Bo explains. "But when you combine all the factors, only one comes out on top — the University of Michigan."

Compared to today's highly intensified recruiting wars, the process of many years ago is somewhat like a typewriter in the modern world of high-tech computerization.

"Most good athletes from the state and around the Midwest just naturally wanted to go to Michigan," explained Don Lund, who won nine letters during his 1942-1944 varsity career.

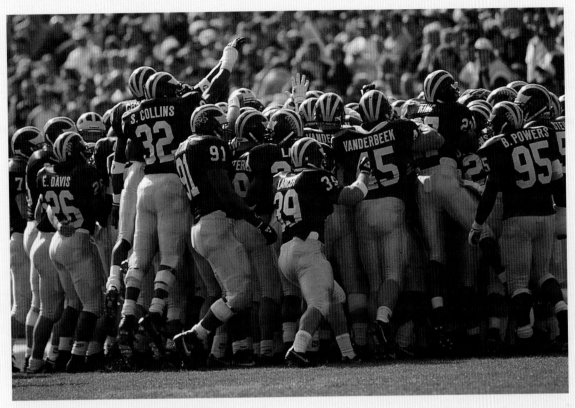

"We must have put some points on the board."

"Mr. Yost or Fritz Crisler might send out a postcard saying they would like you to come to Michigan. A lot of the recruiting was done by local alumni groups. Probably the first time a recruit actually met the coach was in the fall on the field."

Lund graduated from Detroit's Southeastern High School in 1940. In addition to Michigan, he was recruited by Northwestern, Notre Dame, Michigan State, and Yale.

"In my senior year I attended the Michigan Football Bust and Tom Harmon had won the Heisman Trophy," Lund said. "I was so impressed by him and the entire Michigan program. That's when I knew I had to attend."

Competition now for the finest high school talent has assumed a life of its own. That's why the combined excellence of academics and athletics at Michigan is a nuclear weapon in the recruiting wars.

"If a kid wants a quality degree from a great university and also the chance to play for a nationally ranked team, that's a helluva combination to beat," Bo said.

"When you recruit and you go into a school or a home and say 'I'm from the University of Michigan,' you are always welcome. No one throws you out of there. And you always walk in the front door."

One of Bo's proudest recruiting efforts involved Stefan Humphries, an offensive guard out of St. Thomas Aquinas High School in Broward, FL. Humphries became a 1983 All-American. He also was awarded the Big Ten Conference's Medal of Honor for excellence in academics and athletics.

Before Humphries selected Michigan, it had been generally accepted that he would attend Notre Dame.

"I got to know the nun who ran St. Thomas

"Development and training have become a year-round process. Preparation is the key to success."

Aquinas real well," Bo said. "She was a helluva woman.

"She said, 'Bo, I don't want you coming down here and taking one of our kids away from Notre Dame.'

"I said, 'Sister, come on now. Notre Dame cannot give him the academics we can give. He wants biomedical engineering. How do you get that stuff at Notre Dame? He's got the grades to come here academically. You can't just base this decision on religion. We've got more than one Catholic Church in Ann Arbor. And I'll bet you I have as many Catholic players as Notre Dame does.'"

Bo persisted. He did not want to lose an outstanding young man. In an emotional press conference at the high school gymnasium, Humphries stunned a lot of so-called experts when he announced that he had chosen Michigan over Notre Dame.

"A few days later, the sister called me," Bo said. "She said, 'Now do I have tickets for the games up there?' She was a tremendous person."

Humphries also proved to be a tremendous individual. Not only was he a three-year starter, he eventually earned a medical degree.

"Michigan football always has and always will recruit honestly," said Terrell Burton, who served as a longtime assistant under Bo. "We won't go under the table to get that one kid who might make the difference. But we'll win. And we'll win with integrity."

That same philosophy applies to today's program.

"Lloyd Carr and his whole staff have done a marvelous job," Bo said. "Look at the kids who make up the team. They're not just great football players. All these kids have excellent character. And every one of them plays for the team and the University of Michigan. That's the way it's supposed to be. That's the Michigan way!"

"Don Lund (33) and Joe Ponsetto (26) typify what Michigan is all about."

"Two great co-captains in 1983 — Stefan Humphries and John Lott."

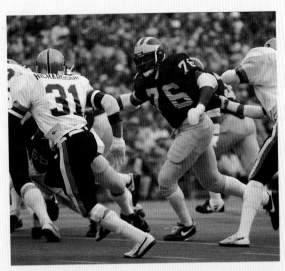

"Those white shirts want no part of Stefan Humphries."

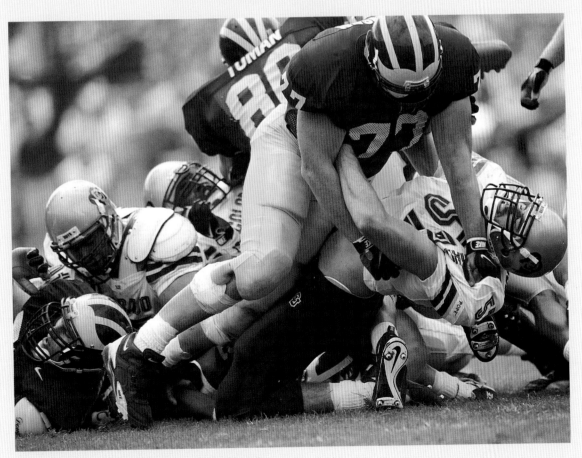

"At Michigan, that's what we call a pancake block."

PRICELESS MEMORIES

For Rick Leach, there are as many warm memories from his Michigan career as there are people who cram into that football stadium for each home game.

There should be, after spending four years (1975-1978) as the starting quarterback.

The warmest memory, though, occurred at the Ohio Stadium in Columbus on November 25, 1978 after Michigan defeated Ohio State, 14-3, for the third straight year.

After the usual postgame hysteria of beating the Buckeyes, Leach sat quietly in front of his locker. All of his physical strength had been left on the field. Except for the upcoming Rose Bowl, Leach had played his last game for Michigan. It was a bittersweet moment for the left-hander who established almost all of the school passing records.

Somehow, through the maze of celebrating supporters outside the Michigan locker room, his father, Richard, Sr., maneuvered his way into the room.

"I was drained...physically and mentally," Leach said. "I looked up and saw my dad walking toward me. When he got to my locker, we sort of looked at each other and then we hugged. Neither one of us said a word. We didn't have to. We communicated more than if we had said a thousand words."

The memory becomes even more precious to Leach with each passing year. That hard-fought victory marked the end of a remarkable four-year run. Both father and son quickly reflected on all the good times.

Leach's father and mother, Nancy, never missed one of their son's games. They still attend all home games and many on the road.

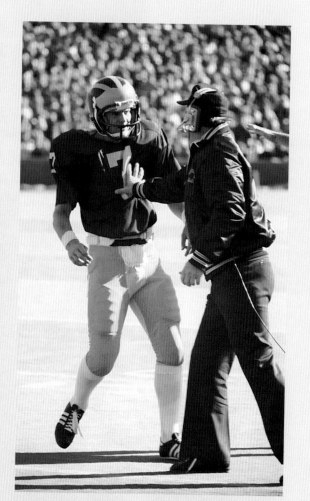

"Rick Leach started 48 consecutive games in four years, more than any other player in Michigan history. He could run that option and take a hit. I'll tell you — that man was tough!"

"Now that I have three sons of my own, I can only imagine the pride my father must have felt," Leach said. "That's something I'll keep for the rest of my life."

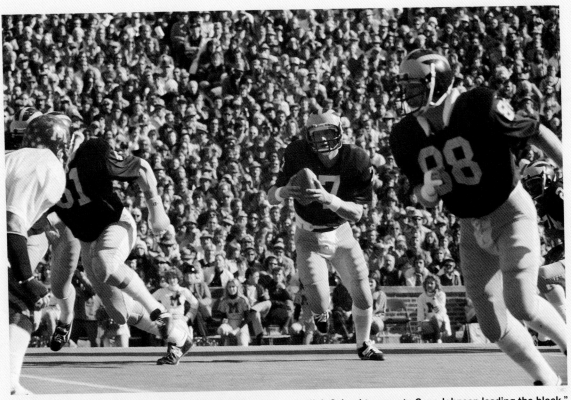

"That's Rick Leach running the option with Flint Southwestern High School teammate Gene Johnson leading the block."

The following spring, Leach became the Detroit Tigers' No. 1 draft pick. He spent nine years in the major leagues.

"When you're playing sports, you sort of get wrapped up in your own little world," he said. "Now that I'm part of the real world, I appreciate even more what the University of Michigan means to me.

"There's a special kind of chemistry and togetherness here. Everyone is part of it. It's not just the athletes. You hear people talk about the Michigan Family and all of it is true. The Michigan Family takes care of its own. It's a pretty good feeling to know that wherever you travel, there's always going to be part of that Michigan Family there to help you if you need it."

Leach left his mark on the Michigan record books. He was one of the finest athletes in university history. Three times he was named All-Big Ten quarterback. In 1978, he earned All-American honors and was named Michigan's and the Big Ten's Most Valuable Player. During his four years, the Wolverines shared three Big Ten championships and compiled an overall 38-8-2 record.

"Bo had such a passion for excellence and the tradition of Michigan Football," Leach said. "Of all the people I've met in sports, he was the greatest motivator I've ever been around. He knew how to get the best out of every player he had. He made you want to succeed. Those are the kinds of lessons that you carry throughout your whole life, even when your playing career is over."

Leach certainly made his coach proud. And the Michigan tradition is richer because of both of them.

EARLY MAIZE AND BLUE BLOOD

Jim Harbaugh is one of those special alums who has tasted all the plums of the Michigan Football tradition.

Before earning All-American honors as quarterback under Bo Schembechler and then going on to star in the National Football League, he grew up in Ann Arbor as a Michigan football fanatic. While his father, Jack, served as one of Bo's assistant coaches from 1972-1979, young Harbaugh went to all the practices starting at just nine-years-old, and served as a ball boy during the games.

"I lived and died with Michigan," Harbaugh said. "There's absolutely nothing on earth like

"And that's Jim Harbaugh — a leader of men!"

"That's Jim Harbaugh when he was one of our ball boys! I must have kicked him out of a hundred practices."

a football Saturday in Ann Arbor. That's what I lived for.

"On Friday nights I never slept. I got so keyed up for the games. I listened to a Bob Ufer record over and over so much that I actually wore it out. I memorized all the words."

Former Michigan All-American quarterback Rick Leach was Harbaugh's boyhood hero.

Harbaugh spent his first two years of high school at Ann Arbor Pioneer. He spent his junior and senior years in California when his family moved there.

Harbaugh was recruited by Arizona and Wisconsin along with a variety of smaller schools. There was no decision to be made

once he was offered a scholarship from Michigan.

"I could never repay Michigan for everything it's done for me and my family," Harbaugh said. "Not just for the opportunity in football, but for everything it's meant to my life. Anyone who has gone to Michigan will tell you the same thing. You don't have to play football to realize that."

Harbaugh did play, though. And he played like few other quarterbacks in Michigan history.

A three-year starter (1984-1986), he earned All-American honors in his senior year. During that season he also was voted Michigan's Most Valuable Player, Big Ten Player of the Year, and finished third in the Heisman voting.

"I received such good coaching at Michigan," Harbaugh said. "From Bo and all the assistants. They taught us how to become men. To this day, whenever anything good or bad happens to me in life I call Bo to get his feelings on the matter. He gets thousands of calls like that from his old players. I don't know if he truly understands how much he means to us."

That burning sense of Michigan tradition he felt as a player is still carried by Harbaugh today.

"When you play for Michigan, you can't help but feel all of the great players and coaches who performed before you," Harbaugh said. "That helped to give you a toughness for not letting them down. And no one ever wanted to let Bo down. He's the kind of person you wanted to do well for."

Harbaugh will never forget the speech Bo delivered to the team before the Wisconsin game in 1984.

"We beat Miami of Florida in the season opener and then got beat by Washington," Harbaugh recalled. "We played Wisconsin the next week. Before the game, Bo gave one of the best speeches I ever heard in my life.

"He said, 'People all over the country are saying that Michigan got MAN-handled by Washington. Can you imagine anyone MAN-handling Michigan? What do we tell guys like McKenzie and Dierdorf and all the guys who went before us?'"

Needless to say, Michigan went out that day and defeated Wisconsin.

Of all Harbaugh's Michigan football memories, one of his fondest came in 1985 after the Wolverines beat Ohio State, 27-17, in Michigan Stadium. After the game, Bo called Harbaugh into his office.

"'Do you realize how much you meant to Michigan today?'" he asked me. "'Do you realize how proud your parents are of you?' I'll never forget that moment."

Nor will Michigan fans ever forget what Harbaugh wove into the fabric of Michigan Football tradition.

ALL IN THE FAMILY

"Don Dufek set the table for his boys by winning the MVP of the 1951 Rose Bowl."

The Dufek family has permanently etched its name in the Michigan Football tradition.

Not once...not twice...but three times.

Don Dufek was a bruising fullback who scored both touchdowns and was named Most Valuable Player in Michigan's 14-6 victory over California in the 1950 Rose Bowl. Later he served as an assistant coach at Michigan.

Don, Jr. was an All-American strong safety and twice earned All-Big Ten honors. His brother, Bill, was a punishing offensive tackle who also was named to an All-Big Ten team.

Dufek played for Bennie Oosterbann. Both his sons played for Bo.

All three families still reside in Ann Arbor. And, of course, they attend all the football games.

"We park in the golf course and tailgate with everyone else," Bill said.

Few fathers have had the special football thrills that the senior Dufek has enjoyed.

"I feel very fortunate in a lot of ways," he said. "I was fortunate to play in a Rose Bowl in my senior year. Then I went to the Rose Bowl as an assistant coach, and that's the hardest because there's so much pressure. Then I got to go there when Billy played under Bo. And finally I went just as a fan. That's the easiest."

Both Dufek boys had to find out more about their father's Michigan heroics from others than they did from their dad.

"He's a very humble man," Bill said. "When my brother and I were kids, we used to wear his helmet and jersey that he got from All-Star games. But it wasn't till we played at Michigan that we found out from others how good he was."

Don, Jr. echoed his brother's feelings.

"One time the University wanted to display the trophy my dad won for being the MVP in the Rose Bowl," he said. "My father had forgotten where he had put it. It was stored away somewhere in the attic."

The Michigan Football tradition was felt by all the Dufeks.

"When I was growing up in Ann Arbor, those Saturdays were the biggest days of the year," Don, Jr. said. "You could buy end zone seats for $1. It was great."

"Billy and Donnie Dufek...when they hit somebody, that guy needed more than an umbrella to protect himself. This is at picture day, otherwise there would have been no umbrella. Mother Pat must have taken that photo."

Bill was always amused at other players when he participated in postseason All-Star games.

"Wherever I went, the guys always wanted to put on my Michigan helmet," he said.

Playing for Bo, the two young Dufeks learned how the Michigan Football tradition helped to mold them into men.

"Bo could take kids from every type of ethnic and social and economic background and mold them into one," Bill said. "I used to joke he treated everyone equally — like dogs.

"Honestly, though, I think Bo sort of symbolized the whole Michigan tradition. Everything is for the team. We've had our share of stars, but the whole experience is to produce excellence from teamwork."

The Dufeks certainly have left their mark on that tradition.

"That beatup nose on Don Dufek was a small price to pay for a victory in the 1951 Rose Bowl."

THE APPLE MAN

To some of the young Michigan players, he's first known as the "Apple Man."

There was a time when Bo was coaching when a couple of his younger men asked, "Who in the hell is the old guy who comes around with apples every Wednesday?"

"Take a look around this field," Bo told his players. "Who's wearing No. 87?"

After a quick look, they discovered no one was.

"That's because the number belongs to HIM," Bo said.

It's Ron Kramer — No. 87. The number was retired after his senior season in 1956.

"There used to be a man named Chestnut

"That's Kramer of Michigan!"

"Grab that ball, Kramer, and take it in for MICH-i-gan."

who brought apples around to us each week," Kramer said. "A while ago I decided maybe it was my turn."

So every Wednesday during the football season, Kramer picks up three bushels of apples — Michigan, of course — and delivers them to the football facility at Schembechler Hall.

He loves it. It gives him the chance to extend that tie to the happiest years of his life.

"There is absolutely no tradition like the Michigan tradition," Kramer says proudly. "A boy who comes here knows he is going to a high class educational institution and

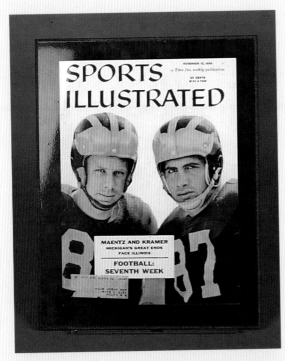

expects the athletic program to reflect those same standards. And he's never disappointed.

"It's impossible to put that feeling of tradition into words. You can't describe it. You feel it. I've been all over the world and there hasn't been a place where I didn't find a Michigan man.

"It's not a case of what the school can give you...it's what you can give back to the school."

Kramer gave back plenty. Not only did he achieve his degree, he also is rightfully regarded as one of the best all-around athletes in Michigan history.

He was a two-time football All-American. He played end on both sides of the ball and also spent time as running back, quarterback, punter, and placekicker.

Coach Bennie Oosterbaan described his blocking and tackling ability as the team's most valuable asset.

"To top off his marvelous physical gifts of size and speed and strength, plus an uncanny coordination, Kramer was one of the fiercest competitors I've ever seen," Oosterbaan said. "Nothing was impossible for him — the impossible was only a challenge."

Kramer also captained the basketball team and was an accomplished high jumper in track. He finished his career with nine varsity letters when freshmen were ineligible.

Kramer's mother, the late Adeline, attended 241 straight Michigan home football games until she died in 1988. She held seats 24 and 25 in row 83 of section 2.

"Everybody knew her there," Kramer said. "It didn't matter if it was pouring rain or snowing, she never left till that game was over. She sat in row 83 — the number I wore for the Detroit Lions; she saw her last game in '87 — the number I wore at Michigan; and she died in '88 — the number I wore for the Green Bay Packers."

Kramer purchased a Michigan brick in his parents' honor near Champions Plaza. It reads — "John & Adeline Kramer, Parents of Ron Kramer."

It's impossible to touch the tradition of Michigan Football without conjuring up warm memories of Ron Kramer.

He still follows the games with the same passion he demonstrated on the field. And he cherishes his weekly Wednesday visits bearing Michigan apples to Schembechler Hall.

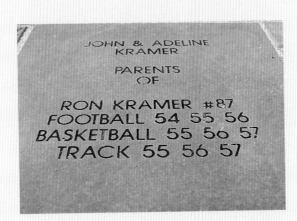

WISTERT...WISTERT... WISTERT

"Al Wistert...he didn't need a face mask."

The Wistert brothers didn't arrive at the University of Michigan wearing No. 11. All three did their part, though, to make it one of the most celebrated numbers in Michigan history. After they left, no one has worn it and no one ever will.

To honor the unprecedented piece of history the Wisterts contributed to the Michigan tradition, No. 11 has been retired.

Francis (Whitey), Albert (The Ox), and Alvin (Moose) all played tackle and all were voted first-team All-American, an accomplishment that has never been duplicated by

three brothers on any level of collegiate competition.

The Wisterts came from Chicago. They were tougher than any midwestern snowstorm and played their position on the line as fiercely as a January blizzard.

"Whitey" paved the way by winning All-American honors for the 1933 Big Ten and

"Al Wistert never forgot his heart belongs to Michigan."

84

"What's better than one Wistert? How about three of them? From left to right: Alvin, Albert, and Francis."

National Championship team. He also was the 1934 Big Ten's Most Valuable Player in baseball and played professionally for Cincinnati.

"The Ox" earned his All-American honor in 1942 when he also was named Michigan's Most Valuable Player. He played nine years for the Philadelphia Eagles and eventually was selected to the National Football Hall of Fame.

"Moose" enjoyed as colorful a personal history as the Wisterts did collectively.

Not only did he not play high school athletics, he did not arrive at the University of Michigan until after serving four years in the Marines in World War II. After one year at Boston University, "Moose" came to Michigan in 1947. At 32, he was the oldest man ever to play for Michigan.

He earned All-American honors in both 1948 and 1949.

No. 11 belongs to the Wisterts. No one can take it from them.

HARMON OF MICHIGAN

In the days of "Ol' 98," there was no contraption like the modern face mask.

It literally was "in-your-face football" and it took a lot of guts to go crashing through a line.

With his square jaw, needle nose, and eye for daylight, that's just the way Tom Harmon liked it. He was "Ol' 98" — Michigan's first

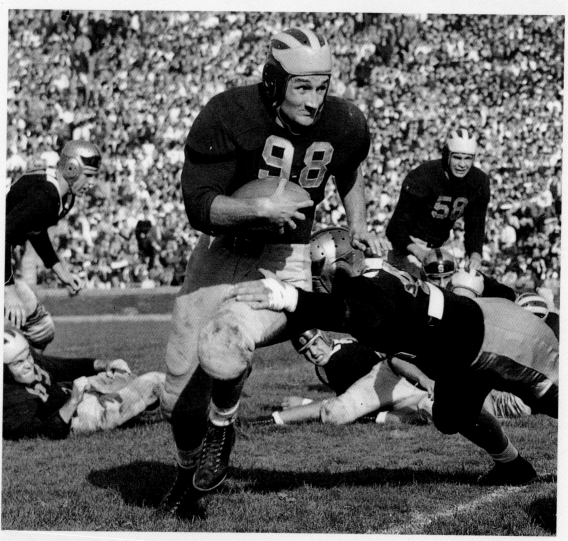

"Harmon of Michigan. No one will ever wear No. 98 again."

"That Heisman belongs to Tom Harmon, one of the greatest players in intercollegiate history."

Heisman Trophy winner and one of the nation's greatest backs of his era.

On the field there was nothing Harmon couldn't do. A two-time All-American halfback, he ran, passed, played defense, punted, and did the placekicking.

Twice he led the nation in scoring. For this three-year (1938-1940) career, Harmon ran and passed for 3,438 yards, threw 17 touchdown passes, kicked 33 extra points and two field goals, and scored 33 touchdowns.

In his Heisman season of 1940, Harmon saved the best for last. Before 73,480 fans at Columbus, he turned in one of the most magnificent individual performances ever by a Wolverine and left the field to a standing ovation even though Michigan crushed Ohio State, 40-0.

In that game, Harmon rushed for 139 yards and two touchdowns. He completed 11 of 12 passes for 151 yards and two touchdowns. He scored four extra points. He intercepted three

"There was NOTHING that man couldn't do."

"Harmon was a great triple threat player — run, pass and kick."

passes, including one for a touchdown. He averaged 50 yards per punt.

That game was a whole season for any other player. But then, Harmon never was just any other player.

Harmon came out of Gary, Indiana to become a Michigan legend and capture every Wolverine heart. The one that captured Harmon's heart was actress Elyse Knox, whom he married. Harmon settled in the Los Angeles area after playing professional foot-

ball and enjoyed a successful broadcast career.

An Air Force fighter and bomber pilot, he rose to the rank of Captain in World War II. Twice his plane was shot down and he walked back to safety. For his military heroics, he was awarded the Silver Star and Purple Heart.

No Michigan player will wear that retired number ever again. No Michigan fan ever will forget it.

"Ol' 98."

LIFE

MICHIGAN'S GREAT HARMON

NOVEMBER 11, 1940 **10** CENTS
YEARLY SUBSCRIPTION $4.50

"That cover tells it all."

STRIKE THE POSE

There were all those acrobatic catches just in the nick of time.

There was the time in the end zone after scoring a touchdown that he "struck the pose."

And always there was that infectious grin that sparkles so bright it makes everyone want to smile.

That was Desmond Howard, Michigan's second Heisman Trophy winner. Howard won the award after his All-American season in 1991.

Howard actually didn't just win it. He ran off with the voting as if he were racing for the end zone on another touchdown romp. He took the Heisman by the second largest margin of victory in the trophy's history.

There may have been better all-around players in Michigan history. Few, however, were as electrifying as the 5-foot-9, 176-pound wide receiver.

Howard was one of those rare players who drew plenty of attention whether or not he was actually part of a play. He was as dangerous as a live hand grenade. His quickness and ability to shake loose in a crowd made him an instant scoring threat even when least expected.

Howard was teamed with Elvis Grbac who also was his quarterback at Cleveland's St. Joseph High.

Howard was the first receiver in Big Ten history to lead the conference in scoring (90) as he set or tied five NCAA records and 12 single-season Michigan marks. Voted Most Valuable Player by his teammates, he set records for most points scored (138), most touchdowns (23), and most consecutive games with a scoring catch (19).

And he did it all with that magnificent smile.

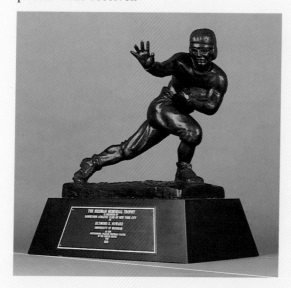

"'The Catch' that won the game and propelled him to Heisman frontrunner."

THE HUMAN HIGHLIGHT FILM

For eternity, Charles Woodson's name will be linked with Tom Harmon and Desmond Howard as Michigan Men who have captured the Heisman Trophy.

Woodson's name is permanently engraved on the imposing bronze statue that symbolizes college football's finest player.

And just as permanently etched in the memories of all Michigan faithful is a kaleidoscope of magical images of dazzling, daring, and dizzying plays brought to life by Woodson in the unforgettable season of 1997.

Not only was Woodson voted the nation's finest player, he was a single-handed human highlight film. To the nation he was an endless script of gravity-defying interceptions, receptions, runs, returns, and good old-fashioned bone-jarring hits.

A sampling:

• A leaping one-handed grab of a Michigan State pass which Coach Lloyd Carr calls "the finest interception I have seen."

• A spine-snapping crunch of a Baylor receiver to signal the nation not to mess with Woodson.

• A 28-yard pass completion to quarterback Brian Griese to shock Wisconsin before the Ohio State showdown.

• A 37-yard reception to set up Michigan's first touchdown against the Buckeyes.

• An end zone leaping interception that featured Michael Jordan-like hang time to stifle Washington State in the Rose Bowl.

"If there was any doubt about who would win the Heisman, this punt return settled it. Just ask Ohio State."

• And his run to the Heisman — a 78-yard punt return for a touchdown to put the stake in Ohio State's heart.

Just as Michigan defied all prognosticators who laughed at the Wolverines' chances of getting through their nightmare schedule

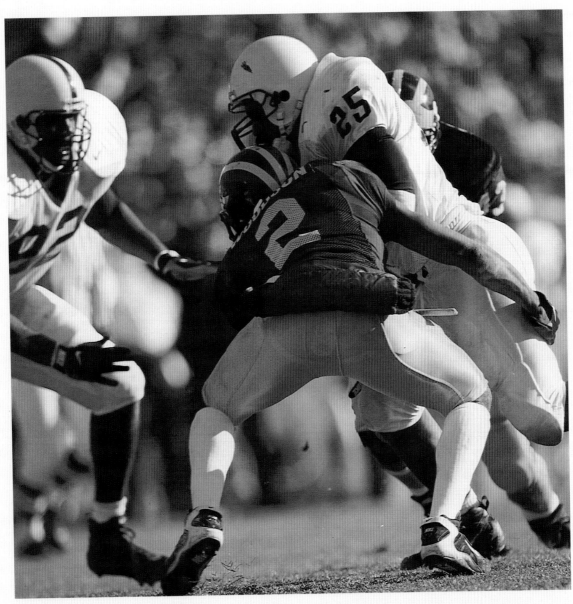

unscathed, Woodson also defied history by becoming the first primarily defensive player to win the Heisman.

And just as all the Wolverines embraced the challenge, so did Woodson.

Throughout his personal parade to history, Woodson never placed individual honors above the goals of the team. Playing unselfishly and operating within the chemistry which Coach Carr created, Woodson worked diligently and led by example.

Consequently, Michigan captured a National Championship and Woodson walked off with the most significant single honor his sport has to offer.

And Wolverine faithful were rewarded with a lifetime of memories that will forever be woven into the fabric of the Michigan Football tradition.

"He looks like a real-life Heisman Trophy."

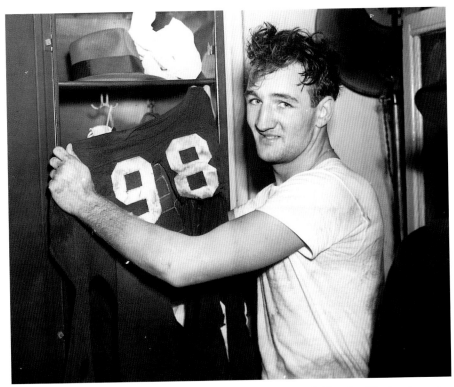

"Judging by that hat, Tom Harmon looked just as good off the field as he did when he was running the ball."

"How about that 'Michigan Man' with his future wife, actress Elyse Knox?"

"Harmon had done it on the field. Now he was signing up to go to war."

"Here's the 1942 team signing a ball for Harmon of Michigan to carry in his plane during the war."

"Jamie Morris was the cutest little runner I ever saw. I only thought he'd be a kick returner. Never judge the size of a man's heart by the size of his body."

"Look at that stance. Look at that hair. That's me."

"That's the old field house and the boys working out."

"William Cunningham — Michigan's first All-American. Do you think times have changed?"

"How about those seats for a game?"

"Tyrone Wheatley — the speed of a tailback and the power of a fullback. How about 235 yards rushing in the 1993 Rose Bowl?"

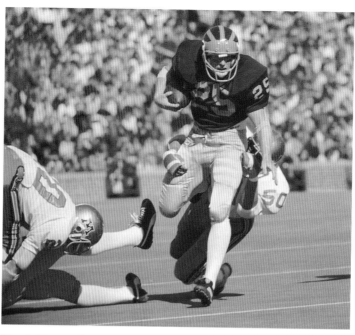

"Rob Lyttle was the most unselfish player I ever had. We moved him from tailback to fullback one year and he never said a word. He just did the job."

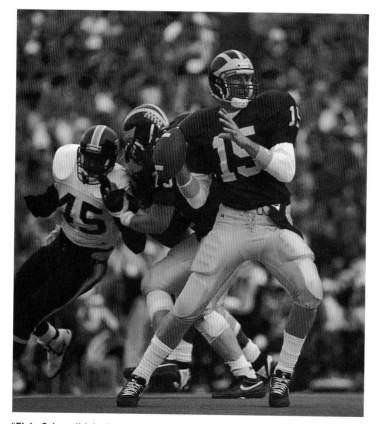

"Elvis Grbac didn't throw in high school. We had to bring him to Michigan to develop him as a passer.

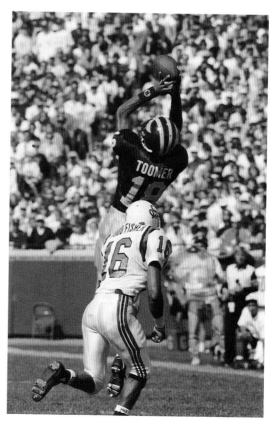

"With a little head start, Amani Toomer could touch the sky."

UFER OF MEE-SHEE-GAN

Bob Ufer was the consummate "homer" when it came to broadcasting Michigan Football. The thing that made him so special was that his passion was real. He was not a phony. He absolutely loved Michigan. And everyone loved him.

He made a three-yard Michigan run sound like a game-winning touchdown. People who listened to him on the radio while watching the game on television might not realize they were watching the same game. That's how openly he wore his love for Michigan.

Rival coaches used to tell me, "I wish we had a guy like that broadcasting our games."

On Fridays before a game, he always taped me for his pre-game show. I'll always remember the trick I played on him before our first game against Notre Dame.

"Oh boy, this is going to be a big game," he said when he walked through my door.

"Ufe, I hate to tell you this," I said.

He got real nervous.

"What's happening...what's happening?" he asked.

"Rick Leach is out," I told him.

His jaw almost hit the floor.

"No, no, no," he said.

I thought he was going to die. I had to tell him I was just kidding. That's how much he loved Michigan. He helped in recruiting. He'd do anything for the University.

He was a good man. I loved him.

"There was nothing Bob Ufer (middle right) loved more than Michigan."

"Jim Smith was our first NFL-type receiver. He had the moves and the hands to go with them."

"The way Calvin Bell gets off his feet Tommy Amaker might be able to use him."

"Ron Johnson was quick...powerful...and I would have loved to have coached him. He finished one year before I arrived. Before he left, he set the Michigan single-game rushing record of 347 yards and scored 5 touchdowns against Wisconsin here on November 16, 1968."

"When you kick a field goal as big as this one, you don't have to see the ball to know it's good. Remy Hamilton kicked this one with two-seconds left to beat Notre Dame, 26-24, in South Bend in 1994. That broke a lot of Irish hearts. Now isn't that too bad?"

A GIVING HERO

One incident best describes what Anthony Carter meant to his teammates and the Michigan Football tradition.

After we beat Washington in the 1981 Rose Bowl, Anthony walked into the coaches' dressing room. He had showered and dressed quickly and left the players' locker room.

"Anthony, you shouldn't be here," I said to him. "You should be over there with all the press and TV reporters."

He looked at me and said, "Coach, I've done enough of that. If I'm not there, they'll have to talk to my teammates."

That's the way Anthony Carter always was. He didn't want to stand in the locker room surrounded by all the press while his teammates, who had played their hearts out, were ignored. He was a legitimate superstar who never wanted that label.

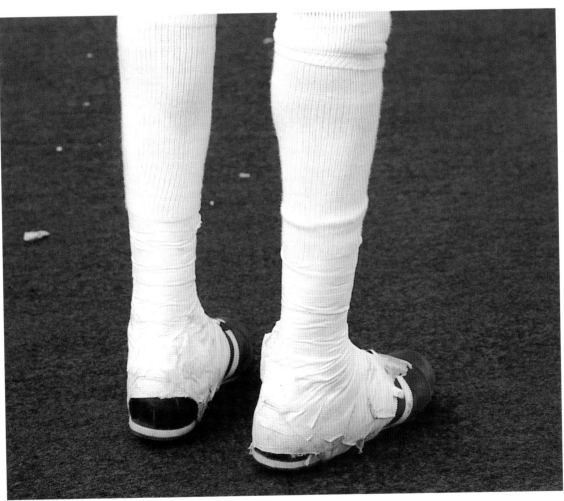

"He wore No. 1 on his jersey. But all you had to do was look at his legs. They were skinny, but man what a big heart!"

"A.C. was a three-time All-American and could break a game wide open quicker than any-body could open a bottle of pop. Number 82 is Dr. Norman Betts leading the blocking."

He had so much talent, but he was the complete team player. He was unbelievably unselfish. Everybody loved him.

The other thing that was so different about Anthony was his toughness. It was unmatched by any other receiver. He was fearless going into the middle to catch a ball. He got hit and knocked around, but he always jumped up. He was never intimidated by secondary backs coming at him.

When he first came to Michigan, we weren't exactly known as a great passing team. On the first day of practice we had our quarterbacks throwing long. It didn't matter how far they over-threw Anthony, he simply ran under the ball and caught it. None of our coaches had ever seen anything like it.

He started making the big play for us even as a freshman. The first time he returned a punt he took it in for a touchdown. Everyone expected a big play from him and he always delivered.

As a freshman in 1979 when he caught that pass with no time left and took it in for a game-winning touchdown, Indiana knew the ball was going to him. They made one mistake. They thought they'd let him catch it and then bring him down. That didn't happen to Anthony Carter with the game on the line.

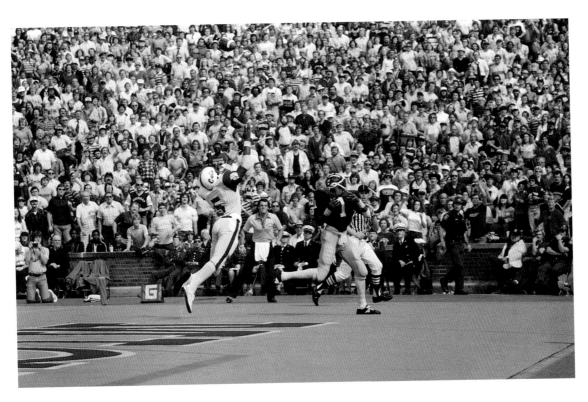

A TRULY "PASSING" TRADITION

"Look at that protection for Todd Collins. That is what every good quarterback needs."

As one tradition welcomes another, the precise moment of transition sometimes is blurred.

There's no mistaking, however, that almost two decades into a pro style quarterback offense the modern Michigan tradition has become a favorite of the league that plays its games on Sundays.

Big-time passers coupled with big play receivers have turned the Michigan program into a fertile feeding system for the NFL.

"It's amazing," Bo reflected. "There's been one after another that have gone on to highly successful professional careers."

The long lines of quarterbacks and wide receivers comprise a "who's who" in the ranks of NFL notables.

Jim Harbaugh, Elvis Grbac, Todd Collins, Brian Griese and Tom Brady were from the throwing side of the ledger. On the receiving

"From the University of Michigan to a Super Bowl Championship, that's a pretty good ride for Tom Brady."

side were Greg McMurtry, Chris Calloway, Desmond Howard, Derrick Alexander, Amani Toomer, Tai Streets, David Terrell and Marquise Walker to name a few.

"And don't forget Anthony Carter," Bo added. "He came along before the transition and might have been the best of them all."

Although the running game must be potent to allow an air attack to realize its potential, the transition has opened a new dimension to the college game.

"When I coached, our game was built on running the ball and the ability to play defense," Bo explained. "Back then, the

"Check out Chris Calloway...eye's open and always on the ball."

option was the trend. Look at all the great teams of the '70s – Alabama, Texas, Nebraska, Ohio State, Michigan. We all ran some version of the option.

"John Wangler was probably the first guy we had who was not an option quarterback. The beautiful part was that he had Anthony Carter waiting for the ball. We ran an option with Jim Harbaugh, but he was basically a drop back passer. We ran the ball and base blocked, but we became more of a play option passing team. And then came Elvis Grbac who was a true drop back passer."

Bo fondly recalls his teams' ability to jam a football clear through the esophagus of any opposition.

"Derrick Alexander sure did that number 1 jersey proud."

"There's no question I wanted to increase our ability to throw the ball," he said. "But I wanted to do it because I knew that no seven men in the box were ever going to stop me from running the ball. If they threw eight or nine up there, I wanted to isolate someone, one-on-one, and get him open. Show me the great teams and I'll show you they can run the

"Just get Tai Streets the football, and he'll take care of the rest."

"John Navarre will leave with all the Michigan passing records."

ball. That's why you hear Lloyd Carr emphasize the importance of the running game."

But times did change. The influence of professional football had a tremendous impact on the college game. Bo also is convinced that changes within the college landscape also had a hand in the offensive transition.

"My theory is that the constant reduction in football scholarships forced teams to do things that do not require as much physical strength," he explained. "It's a lot easier to pass than to line up out there and base block an opponent. It's forced a lot of teams to turn to a game that's more like a basketball fire drill."

Michigan modified its philosophy to capitalize on both power and athleticism.

"The success of any quarterback is enhanced by the ability of his receivers to make big plays," Bo said. "A great receiver really has an impact on your offense. The big thing is his ability to run after the catch."

Fortunately for Michigan, the line of successful receivers is as long as the one at quarterback.

With John Navarre poised to shatter every Michigan passing record and with youngsters such as Matt Guiterrez and Clayton Richard waiting in the wings, the quarterback legacy rests in good hands.

Receivers such as Braylon Edwards, Jason Avant, Steve Breaston and Carl Tabb are ready to make the second part of the equation just as impressive.

And it won't resemble in the least any similarity to a "basketball fire drill."

"Look it in Braylon, look it in!"

"Hold on Maurice!"

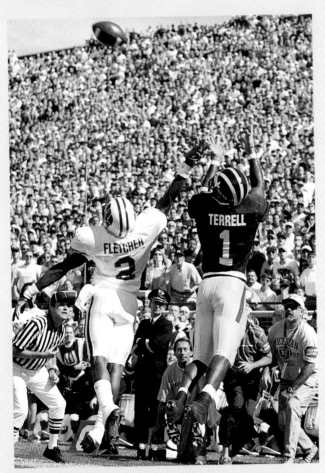

"Catching that ball isn't easy unless you're David Terrell."

THE PRIVILEGE OF MICHIGAN

To me, no coach in America asks a man to make any sacrifice.

He requests just the opposite,

Live clean, come clean, think clean,

That he stop doing all the things that destroy him physically,

Mentally, and morally,

And begin doing all the things that make him keener, finer,

And more competent.

— Fielding H. Yost

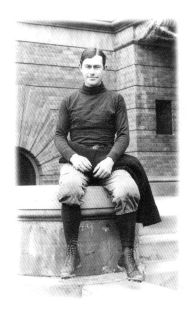

---

hen I first came to Michigan, I brought my assistant coaches with me from Miami of Ohio.

Miami is a good university. Good educational institution. Good athletic program.

Suddenly, though, we were in the big time. As a matter of fact, there was no place bigger than the University of Michigan.

There was the tradition. There were all those great players that had made all that glorious history here. There was that beautiful big stadium.

The locker rooms, at that time, were in Yost Field House. The funny part about it was that the coaches' room was no bigger than an ordinary kitchen. We had rickety, rotten folding chairs to sit on. We hung our clothes on spikes that were nailed into two-by-fours.

One of the coaches said we had 10 times better dressing facilities back at Miami.

"Wait a minute, men," I told them.

"Did you ever sit in the same chair that Fielding H. Yost and Fritz Crisler did? No you didn't.

"Did you ever hang your clothes on the same spike as Harry Kipke and Bennie Oosterbaan did? No you didn't.

"THAT'S the difference between Michigan and every other university in the United States of America. And DON'T you forget it."

Coaching football at the University of Michigan is a very demanding position. What you always must remember, though, it is not a job.

It is a PRIVILEGE.

"That's the 1898 team with Coach Gustave Ferbert (upper right, back row)."

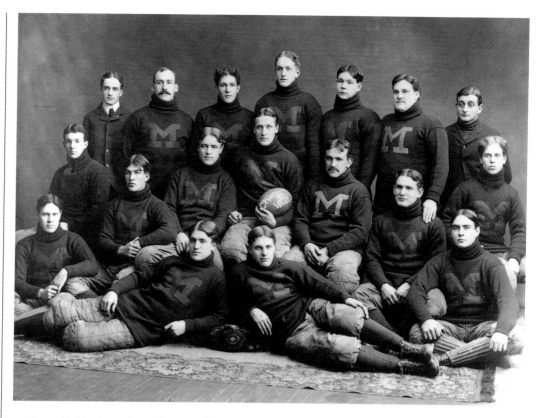

Since 1901, there have been only 10 head football coaches at Michigan, and a couple of the early ones were only on board for a few years.

That's an awfully small number for a program more than a hundred years old. And there's a very good reason for it.

The University takes tremendous pride in placing its tradition into exactly the right hands. When a man is accepted for the position of head coach here, that is an honor. You don't see Michigan coaches politicking for any other job.

That's because all of us knew the same thing — we were privileged to hold the BEST football head coaching job anywhere in the United States of America.

Just watch how some college coaches play musical chairs. Sometimes it's the coaches who are always on the lookout to make another move. Sometimes it's the schools who make the move before a coach has a chance.

That doesn't happen at Michigan. No coach in his right mind is going to shop for flowers when he's already living smack in the middle of the most beautiful garden in the country.

There are a lot of outstanding universities all over the country. There are a number of successful football programs.

When you combine academic excellence with consistent football superiority, though, I believe there is no other school that measures up to the standards of the University of Michigan.

It's impossible to coach at Michigan without feeling the presence of all the great ones who will always remain part of the tradition.

Fielding Yost, for instance, was a man so far ahead of his time, we still haven't caught up to him today.

Can anyone imagine his vision to build a facility like Michigan Stadium way back in 1927?

"Talk about legends, that's Fielding H. Yost (right) with the great Walter Camp, University of Chicago coach, at a 1903 game. I wish I could have coached in one of those hats."

People thought he was crazy to build a stadium that would hold 72,000 people back then. And he had it constructed so that it can accommodate 130,000. He envisioned the day when Michigan Football would demand that number. And he was right.

He didn't stop with just the stadium. He built the country's first collegiate field house. He built an intramural facility to house athletics for the entire student body. And he built a golf course that ranks among the best at all universities.

Yost was a true visionary. He also was one of the most successful coaches in the history of intercollegiate football. He won 165 of 204 games. In 1901, he led Michigan to the first Rose Bowl championship and the school's first national title.

Fritz Crisler was a totally different personality than Yost. He also was brilliant and his

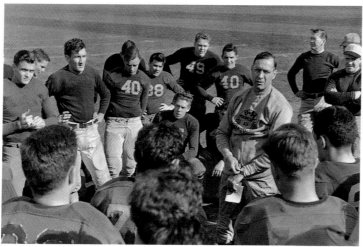

"Fritz Crisler's impromptu meetings were classics."

"You only had to tell Jim Harbaugh once."

contributions to the Michigan tradition are felt today.

Crisler was the foremost national authority on college football rules. He was the originator of two-platoon football. And in 1938, he designed the famous maize-and-blue winged helmet that still remains the most distinctive headgear in football — college or professional!

Every coach privileged to lead Michigan Football had a little different personality and brought a little different approach to the program.

But we all share a couple of qualities. Each coach had a specifically designed program. In his own way, each taught discipline. And just as important, each coach felt a sense for the tradition that the previous ones and all the players established so many years ago.

The tradition of Michigan in academics and football is a powerful recruiting tool. There are other great academic institutions. There are other outstanding football programs.

But no other school in America combines the two as well as Michigan. The University and its tradition is the greatest recruiting weapon any coach could ask for.

In order to be successful in coaching over a long period of time, you had better enjoy

young people. You better enjoy teaching them both on and off the field.

There's pressure to win at any Division-I football program. In fact, I believe there is more pressure now than at any time in our history.

The great coaches, though, create their own special kind of pressure. It's the pressure they feel for making sure all those young players walk away from the program as men once their playing career is finished.

If a coach can help to properly shape the character of those young men to last a lifetime, then that coach was successful regardless what the won-lost record reads.

Every one of those men who coached at Michigan left a lasting impression on each young life he touched. Each coach did so because the Michigan Football program has been founded on honesty and integrity since the first time a ball was kicked.

When I look back during my tenure here, I know there were times when we might have won a couple more games or finished higher in the rankings by picking up a certain player. The price, though, was breaking the rules.

That was NOT going to happen at Michigan. It never happened then and it will not happen now.

Fielding Yost could not have explained the essence of coaching any better than when he said "No coach in America asks a man to make any sacrifice...He requests just the opposite...Live clean, come clean, think clean."

That says it all.

THAT'S the long string that continues to run through all the football coaches at the University of Michigan.

"Youth clinics were always fun, and who could imagine who might be the next Michigan star."

THE ARCHITECT OF TRADITION

FIELDING H. YOST
1901-1923, 1925-1926
(165-29-10)

"Yost was a hands-on coach. He liked to lead by example. Look at him move that ball."

Fielding H. Yost was a visionary long before he put his law degree on the shelf to become, arguably, the architect of big-time college football.

Prior to realizing his dream of making the University of Michigan the premier athletic complex in the country, though, he was an equally magnificent football coach.

For his time, there was none better.

"He was a great coach," Bo said. "It's hard to say what the competition was like back then, but he was the best of whatever it was."

That's as understated as Bo saying he "sort of" enjoys a Michigan victory over Ohio State.

Yost was a professor of football who believed the game taught character. It showed young men how to live properly. He did not believe in drinking, smoking, or carousing. He taught his players that abstinence from such practices is not a sacrifice, but rather the proper way to live.

"He always taught by example," recalled the late Kip Taylor who scored the first touchdown in Michigan Stadium in 1927. He was a freshman and practiced under Yost during the legend's last coaching season in 1926.

"He'd do little things to make sure everyone was prepared," Taylor said. "One day he took all the ends to the goal line and stepped back and forth over the line several times. Then he looked at us and said, 'You can run

"Willie Heston — one of Fielding Yost's first recruits in 1904 turned out to be one of Michigan's greats."

From 1901-1923, and again in 1925-1926, Yost-led Michigan teams set the standards for major college football.

From 1901-1905, Michigan played 56 consecutive games without a loss. That string included winning streaks of 29 and 26 games. In those five seasons, Michigan outscored its opponents, 2,821 to 42.

"The numbers were awesome," Bo said. "But he was a defensive coach. That's what made him so great. All great coaches are defensive coaches."

Yost finished with a 165-29-10 record and won 10 Big Ten titles in a span of 15 years. He also led Michigan to a 49-0 rout over Stanford in the first Rose Bowl in 1901.

"Look at those eyes on Germany Schulz. Try staring at those from across the line."

A TOAST TO YOST FROM COAST TO COAST

YOST
A MICHIGAN INSTITUTION

"THE OLD MAN"

... It's a Great Big Meeshegan Day

OCTOBER 19, 1940   ANN ARBOR, MICHIGAN

He also was a genuinely romantic, almost make-believe, character who commanded his share of the national sporting spotlight in the era of such giants as Babe Ruth. In fact, legendary writer Ring Lardner once said that Yost actually possessed more personality than Ruth.

And Yost wasn't afraid to talk about himself in a fashion where everybody listened. He loved to talk. And he was always prepared to expound on his beloved "Meeshegan."

"He'd talk to anybody," Taylor said. "He'd walk up-and-down State Street and talk football to anybody who'd listen. There'd be tobacco juice dripping down his cheek and his hat would be half off his head, but he'd talk about the game. He loved football. And he loved Michigan."

Howard Wikel, who played from 1943-47, was a boy in his father's pharmacy on University when Yost regularly visited.

"Mr. Yost would come into the store and sit at a little table near the door," Wikel recalls. "As students came in, he'd grab them by the arm. He'd say, 'Sit down here me boy...I want to explain something to you.'"

Yost then would diagram plays using knives and forks and salt and pepper shakers as imaginary players.

over this line a hundred times and it doesn't mean a thing if you don't have that little brown thing in your hands.' It was details...details...details with Mr. Yost."

Yost used the forward pass in 1910 — two years ahead of Knute Rockne, who is generally credited with its inception. In addition, Yost created the position of linebacker with one of his prize pupils — All-American Germany Schulz.

More than anything, Yost taught preparedness as if it were a religion.

"Many have the will to win, but few have the will to prepare," was one of his credos.

So zealous was Yost about preparation that he often put on pads to demonstrate proper blocking and tackling techniques.

Yost transcended his role of coach and visionary who built the Michigan Stadium, Yost Field House, the Michigan Golf Course and the Intramural Building.

"Let me tell you about Howard Wikel. If you want to know anything about Michigan Football, Ann Arbor or just about anything, you better ask Howard."

"Mr. Yost looked like the big-time executive in his new office."

"Then he'd give lessons on the Civil War," Wikel said. "He was a very scholarly person on the war."

Yost spoke with a touch of West Virginia accent and used it to his advantage while spinning his yarns.

"He spoke in stories," Taylor said. "He illustrated everything he talked about with a story. And everybody loved it."

Even in his advancing years, everyone but his closest friends referred to him as Coach or Mr. Yost.

"You had to really know him to call him by his first name," Taylor said. "Even though he was as down-to-earth as a bushel of apples, people just naturally spoke to him with great respect."

Almost a century after first arriving in Ann Arbor, Yost still enjoys the respect accorded a legitimate legend.

He was a first and only. He remains the revered Mr. Yost.

A CRAFTSMAN KNOWN AS CRISLER

HERBERT O. (FRITZ) CRISLER
1938-1947
(71-16-3)

Images of Fritz Crisler range from majestic to aloof.

"There was a majesty about him," said Howard Wikel, who was a reserve halfback on his teams. "There was a certain charm. He could have been an actor, a doctor, or anything he would have wanted to be."

After graduating from the University of Chicago with a degree in psychology, Crisler decided against medical school to pursue a career in coaching.

"At the University of Chicago, Fritz Crisler was quite a player himself."

"He didn't allow people to get too close to him," said Don Lund, one of Michigan's finest all-around athletes who played fullback for Crisler. "Yet after each game, he'd go around to all the players and put his arm around them. If we lost, he'd encourage us to get 'em next week.'"

Crisler was unforgivably meticulous. He never allowed coincidence to carve his destiny. He was the master of design and carefully sculpted everything within his influence.

"Fritz took that 1947 National Champion team to the Rose Bowl and proceeded to hammer USC, 49-0."

"I don't care how well you knew him," Wikel said. "You didn't say hello to him until he said something first. That's just the way it was."

While some regarded Crisler's personality as being somewhat aloof, he was consumed by the smallest detail in his pursuit of Michigan excellence.

His legacy to the Michigan Football tradition transcends his 10-year record of 71-16-3.

It was Crisler in his first year who introduced the famous winged helmets in 1938. Until then, Michigan's helmets were black. Crisler sought distinction. He also felt the design would help facilitate his single-wing offense that demanded speed and deception.

It was Crisler who introduced the two-platoon system when Michigan played top-ranked Army on October 12, 1945 in Yankee Stadium. The inception revolutionized college football.

It also was Crisler who led Michigan back into national football prominence. During his tenure as coach, Michigan finished lower than second in conference play only twice.

Crisler capped his coaching career by directing Michigan to a 49-0 rout of Southern California in the 1948 Rose Bowl to finish an unbeaten season as the national champion.

It was that team that nicknamed Crisler "The Lord."

No disrespect was intended. In fact, it was done out of respect for the way Crisler was always thoroughly prepared and seemed never to overlook even the most minute detail.

"He was always in control," said Bump Elliott who played halfback on that national championship team and later coached at Michigan. "He was uncompromising, but always with good reason. He didn't demand respect, he earned it."

Crisler's preparation was as thorough as the most complex mathematical equation. Each move was orchestrated. Even for

"The note from Harmon sort of sums up the way all of Crisler's players felt. He was a coach...a teacher...a leader...a man."

practices, he used handwritten notes in red and blue pencil.

His pregame and halftime speeches to his teams were delivered with theatrical flair.

"He had a unique commanding personality that gained the absolute attention and respect of those in his presence," said Pete Elliott, who played on that 1947 team and also the 1948 national champion team.

"We would wait for and listen to his every word even to the point of his pauses being dramatic and meaningful."

In his own singular style, Crisler had the ability to motivate like a Sunday morning TV preacher. He never raised his voice. He never cursed. He was clinically articulate. His eyes were like lasers and communicated as well as his words.

"He got the nickname 'Gimlet Eye' from the way that his stare could affect anyone

"That single wing play, 22-power, could take the ball off the flank with double teams inside and outside."

who was the recipient of the stare," said Tom Kuzma who played two years for him.

There was the celebrated incident when All-American halfback Bob Chappuis injured his hamstring while practicing for the 1948 Rose Bowl. While Chappuis lay on the ground, Crisler calmly looked down.

"Good thing it didn't happen to someone who could run," Crisler said with cold deliberation.

Crisler, of course, was concerned for his star. It was merely his way of motivating Chappuis along with showing his team that it could survive adversity.

"I don't know about the rest of the guys, but I felt a lot better after he said that," said Bruce Hilkene who captained that team. "He wanted to show everyone that this was a team effort."

Chappuis also understood what Crisler was doing. And Chappuis responded exactly as his coach hoped he would. He threw for 188 yards and two touchdowns. He also carried the ball 13 times for 91 yards.

Norma Bentley was Crisler's longtime secretary. In the early '90s, Chappuis visited her in an Ann Arbor nursing home. It wasn't until then that he discovered how concerned Crisler had been.

"She told me that Coach Crisler really was worried I wouldn't be able to play in that Rose Bowl," Chappuis said. "That did make me feel good."

Crisler's gift for motivation was unchallenged.

"His pregame pep talks were fabulous," said Al Wistert. "Before the Michigan State game one year he said, 'Nobody ever heard of Michigan State before they beat us. You made them. Now I want you to go out there and break them!'

"Against Minnesota one year he said, 'This game will take all you've got — 60-minutes of unrelenting everlasting pressure — 60-minutes of sacrifice and a lifetime to remember.'"

Wistert also remembers how Crisler was relentless in reminding his men to play and live properly:

"Often he reminded us — 'Remember you are Michigan men. You represent a great university. Don't ever do anything on or off the field of play which might tarnish this revered name — the University of Michigan.'"

For reasons only Crisler knew for sure, however, Crisler preferred to keep his distance. Not only from his players, but also from all but a handful of his closest friends.

After his coaching career, Crisler remained as Athletic Director until his retirement in 1968. Because of his unmatched knowledge of rules and his discipline for details, he was regarded as one of the nation's most influential administrators.

Although reluctantly, even the legendary Woody Hayes acknowledged Crisler's stature. Bo served as an assistant to Hayes at the time.

"It got to Woody," Bo said. "He used to say 'Crisler runs the whole damn conference...A damn guy from Michigan...But he's one smart son of a gun.'"

Crisler was an enigma. But he also left footprints on the Michigan tradition that will remain a century from now.

A TEAM FOR THE AGES

They were called the "Mad Magicians." Who knows for sure if they had the most pure talent? Everyone knows for certain, though, that no other college football team in the country performed at a higher level.

At the time, they were so young. Now...several of them are gone.

Some had served their country in World War II. Others would be called to fight in the Korean War only a few years later.

The glories of that team have withstood the test of time. More than a half-century has passed since that 1947 Michigan team went undefeated, including a 49-0 Rose Bowl rout over the University of Southern California to finish as national champion.

Lunar landings, a presidential assassination, an even deadlier Asian war,

"Bob Chappuis was big-time. Michigan belongs on the cover of *Time*."

"Here's the backfield: (left to right) Bump Elliott, Howard Yerges, Jack Weisenburger, and Bob Chappuis."

"Now that's styling...Bump Elliott and Bob Chappuis with Hollywood star Marlene Dietrich at the 1948 Rose Bowl."

and a technological revolution all have followed that little precious sliver of time that once seemed as though it would never end.

It was the final coaching season for the legendary Fritz Crisler. Like a veteran Broadway performer, he sensed it was the perfect time for his final performance.

The closeness of that team bonded teammates for life. So much so that every five years all remaining members gather for a reunion. Ann Arbor hosted the first nine. For their 50th anniversary, team members planned something special. In 1992, they decided to

meet in Pasadena at the 1998 Rose Bowl.

"What a miraculous turn of events for the 1997 team to be in the same situation as we were," said All-American halfback Bob Chappuis.

Just as its predecessor from a half-century ago, the 1997 team capped off an undefeated season with a victory in the Rose Bowl to finish as national champion.

"There are so many wonderful memories," Chappuis said. "But the Rose Bowl victory probably symbolizes everything.

"The whole picture doesn't really hit you

"Look at that 1947 squad. You can't run the kind of offense they did without tremendous discipline and deception."

until years later. There aren't too many people in the world who can sit around in their pajamas and robe at night and say that they played for an undefeated team that won the Rose Bowl and finished as the national champion. It takes time to really appreciate all of that. Those young men of 1997 don't even know yet just how much they accomplished."

Certainly that 1947 squad had talent. Chappuis and Bump Elliott earned All-American honors. They had plenty of support from players like Bob Mann, Bruce Hilkene, Dominic Tomasi, J.T. White, Stu Wilkins, Bill Pritula, Dick Rifenburg, Howard Yerges, and Jack Weisenburger, among others.

All admit, though, there may have been more talented teams.

"We didn't have the greatest players," Chappuis said. "But Coach Crisler was able to get us to put it altogether and always perform as a team. He always stressed one thing — you had to play better than you know how. Push the other team in the direction you want it to go and don't give up."

That 1947 squad was a perfect reflection of the discipline Crisler always practiced and preached.

"He asked each player to dedicate his efforts to playing football each day one percent better than the previous day," Chappuis said. "He said, 'if you will collectively do this, I will guarantee you now that you will be part of a winning football program.'"

Chappuis calls Crisler "The epitome of dignity."

And that's the way his teams always performed.

While his health permitted, Crisler regularly

June 4, 1973

There are times when the heart is too full for utterance and being with you on your 25th reunion, for me, was one of those times. Even had I been gifted or adequately endowed to express my true feelings any effort would have fallen far short. My human speech would have been naught, my human testimony inadequate, my human estimates futile. Only my silent thoughts fruitful, my silent meditations sacred.

As we travel down the weary path of life thru the garden of our memories no doubt the echoes of yesteryears cheers will become dim, the winners wreaths may wither, the blue in our victory ribbons may fade, trophies may become tarnished, the gleam of our medals lose luster, but the emotional experiences of joy and elation, heartaches and disappointments can never be shared by others. Robust friendships were created. None was lukewarm but all very alive and everlastingly vivid.

These friendships, thru sunshine and shadows, will stand forever as a brilliant beacon high in the halls of our memories framed in majestic reverence.

May good fortune always smile on you and yours, all ways.

Your Old Coach with abiding affection

"Fritz loved all his boys. But that 1947 squad was special. He taught them always to stick together. Isn't this some kind of letter for their 25th reunion?"

attended the five-year reunions of that 1947 squad. Shortly after the 25th reunion in 1973, each member of the team received a letter from their coach expressing his feelings for "his boys" which he rarely displayed.

"I framed it and have it hanging on a wall in my house," Chappuis said. "Sometimes I look at it and it still brings tears to my eyes."

THE LEADERS OF MEN

In spite of being more than a century old, only a handful of men have been chosen to lead the storied Michigan Football program.

MIKE MURPHY and FRANK CRAWFORD

(1891, 4-5-0 record) were the first official coaches. Prior to their appointment, the Michigan football program operated for 11 seasons without a coach.

Crawford initiated Michigan's first advance schedule.

FRANK E. BARBOUR

(1892-1893, 14-8-0) led Michigan on a then-ambitious 12 and 10 game schedule. In 8 of his 14 victories, Michigan posted shutouts.

WILLIAM L. McCAULEY

(1894-1895, 17-2-1) was a Princeton graduate and Michigan medical school student when he was named coach. Michigan's 12-4 victory over Cornell in 1894 marked the first time in collegiate football history that a western school defeated an established power from the east.

WILLIAM D. WARD

(1896, 9-1) also was a Princeton graduate. His team allowed only 11 points all season.

GUSTAVE H. FERBERT

(1897-1899, 24-3-1) became coach after the student-alumni advisory board determined only former Michigan students could coach football. An 1897 graduate, Ferbert led Michigan to its first Big Ten title in 1898.

LANGDON (BIFF) LEA

(1900, 7-2-1) was a Princeton graduate and took over after the former students-only rule had been rescinded. A strict disciplinarian, Lea posted a rule on the wall of the gymnasium stating the word "can't" is not in the football vocabulary.

FIELDING H. YOST

(1901-1923, 1925-1926, 165-29-10) remains the first among Michigan coaching legends. Known as the "Point-a-Minute" teams, Yost-led squads played 56 straight games without a loss from 1901-1905. In those five years, the Wolverines outscored their opponents 2,821 to 42.

The 1901 team went 10-0 and won the Big Ten title before routing Stanford, 49-0, in the first Rose Bowl. Michigan won the national championship in 1901, 1902, 1903, and 1904. Under Yost, Michigan won 10 Big Ten titles and 20 of his players were named All-American.

Yost served as Director of Athletics from 1921-1941. Under Yost's vision, the University built Michigan Stadium, an 18-hole Alister MacKenzie-designed golf course, the nation's first intramural sports building, and the nation's first multi-purpose field house now known as the Yost Ice Arena.

GEORGE LITTLE

(1924, 6-2-0) was a defensive-minded coach and his team shut out opponents in five of its six victories. He had served as Yost's top assistant for two years and left Michigan to become Athletic Director at the University of Wisconsin.

ELTON E. (TAD) WIEMAN

(1927-1928, 9-6-1) was a three-season star for the Wolverines at tackle and fullback, where he earned all-conference honors. Wieman also earned Phi Beta Kappa honors for his classroom achievements.

HARRY G. KIPKE

(1929-1937, 46-26-4) was Michigan's first nine-letterman from football, basketball, and baseball. He was one of the nation's greatest kickers and was named an All-American halfback.

From 1930 through 1933, Michigan won four straight Big Ten titles and was named national champion in 1932 and 1933. Kipke, Yost, and Bo are the only coaches to have led Michigan to four consecutive conference championships.

HERBERT O. (FRITZ) CRISLER

(1938-1947, 71-16-3) led consistently disciplined and superior teams. Only twice during his ten-year career did Michigan finish lower than second in the conference.

Crisler was an offensive-minded coach whose innovations piled up yards. His .805 winning percentage ranks him second in school history behind Yost (minimum 50 games). Before turning his full-time attention to his position of Athletic Director, Crisler's last game was a 49-0 rout of Southern California in the 1948 Rose Bowl to clinch the national title.

BENNIE G. OOSTERBAAN

(1948-1958, 63-33-4) became Michigan's first three-time All-American football player. He won three letters in football, basketball, and baseball.

Following his graduation in 1928, he turned down contracts from professional baseball and football organizations in order to join the Michigan coaching staff. He had a brilliant mind for offense and coached backs and ends for Crisler.

In 1948, he guided the Wolverines to a 9-0 record and a national championship.

CHALMERS W. (BUMP) ELLIOTT

(1959-1968, 51-42-2) holds the rare distinction of both coaching and playing for Michigan teams that won a Big Ten championship and a Rose Bowl.

In 1964, he directed Michigan to a 9-1 record and a 34-7 victory over Oregon State in the Rose Bowl. As an All-American on the Wolverines' national championship team of 1947, he was called the greatest right halfback Crisler had ever seen.

Under Elliott, Michigan produced five All-Americans.

GLENN E. (BO) SCHEMBECHLER

(1969-1989, 194-48-5) has more wins than any other coach in Michigan history. His teams won or tied 13 Big Ten titles. He guided 17 Michigan teams to bowl games, including 10 Rose Bowls. Under Bo, 17 Michigan teams finished in the wire services' Top Ten. In addition to his coaching duties, Bo served as Athletic Director from 1988-1990.

GARY O. MOELLER

(1990-1994, 44-13-3) guided Michigan to four bowl victories in five years, including the 1993 Rose Bowl. Under Moeller, Michigan won three Big Ten championships and had five finishes in the nation's top 20. Michigan also set a Big Ten record by winning 19 straight conference games between 1990-1992.

LLOYD CARR

(1995-present) has delivered more than a national championship to the University of Michigan. He has enhanced the legacy of football excellence through traditional Michigan trademarks – commitment, integrity and team unity. His unselfish program perfectly reflects the foundation upon which the Michigan tradition is based.

Through his first eight years, Carr's Wolverines posted a 76-23 record. In 1997, Michigan set a school record with a 12-0 mark and its first national championship since 1948.

Carr has been part of the Michigan program since 1980, when he started as an assistant under Bo. He was named Interim Head Coach before the start of the 1995 season and was made the 17th permanent Head Coach on November 13 of that year.

Carr was named National Coach of the Year in 1997. Based upon his commitment to the university, the best may be still to come.

THE ELLIOTT LEGACY

No one captures the essence of Bump Elliott better than Jim Conley.

"He was born to be on a Wheaties box," said the 1964 Michigan captain whose team went on to crush Oregon State, 34-7, in the 1965 Rose Bowl under Coach Elliott.

With his Huck Finn looks and Will Rogers personality, Elliott could charm Ebenezer Scrooge into playing Santa Claus.

"Can you imagine any parent of a prospective recruit not wanting to entrust their boy to Bump when he went off to college?" asks Don Lund, another former Michigan standout.

More importantly, Elliott backed up that All-American image with an All-American playing career before taking over the reigns at his alma mater.

Under Fritz Crisler, Elliott helped to lead

"That's Bump and Pete. If they aren't the picture of the All-American boys then you don't like apple pie."

Michigan to the first of back-to-back national championships in 1947. Elliott played right halfback and Bob Chappuis was at left. Both were named All-Americans.

During that season, just two years after returning from overseas duty with the Marines, Elliott led the conference in scoring with 54 points. He also was named Most Valuable Player in the conference.

"He was the greatest right halfback I have ever seen," Crisler once said.

One of Elliott's teammates was his brother, Pete. Both were two-way standouts and comprise one of the most celebrated names in Michigan history.

After serving as an assistant in 1957 and 1958 under Bennie Oosterbaan, Elliott took over as head coach for the 1959 season. He guided the Wolverines to the Rose Bowl victory in 1965.

"There was nothing you could dislike about Bump," Conley said. "He was a great teacher and leader. More importantly, he was a straight shooter. He was so honest."

After that Rose Bowl victory, the Wolverines scuffled for the next three seasons.

"Bump was a terrific coach," Conley said. "Sometimes people don't realize how tough it is to follow a couple of legends like Crisler and Oosterbaan."

Before leaving, however, Elliott assembled a championship team in-waiting. His 1968 team finished the year with an 8-2 record and was ready for Bo to ride them to a Big Ten championship and another Rose Bowl appearance the next season.

"I always joke with Bo that we helped to set

"Going from player to coach at Michigan had to be some kind of special feeling for Bump."

the table for him," Conley cracked. "But I think he had a pretty good idea of what he could do."

During his coaching career, Elliott faced brother Pete, who had taken over the head position at Illinois.

The Elliott name will forever live as a major part of the Michigan tradition.

137

FOREVER BLUE

For Bennie Oosterbaan, there was no better place on earth than the University of Michigan.

It had always been his little piece of paradise from the time he was one of the school's most gifted all-around athletes until he died following a distinguished coaching career.

Perhaps no one cherished the Michigan spirit as much as Oosterbaan. His gift for eternity was provided by his protégé who was as equally athletically gifted and whose love for the University remains unchallenged.

"It was Bennie's wish to always be part of the University," explained former All-American Ron Kramer whose No. 87 was retired by Oosterbaan.

"Before he died we discussed every detail. We did everything with dignity and with the intention of allowing a great man to enjoy his reward for eternity."

Kramer tenderly placed Oosterbaan's ashes in all the places his old coach held dearest to his heart. He placed some near the stadium tunnel and all around the field where Oosterbaan played as a three-time All-American end. He placed some around Yost Field House where he starred on the basketball court. And he placed some around the baseball diamond where Oosterbaan also was a standout.

Oosterbaan had several opportunities to play sports professionally. Instead, he decided never to leave Michigan. Nothing gave him greater happiness than coaching for his life's passion.

"Bennie was Michigan," Kramer said. "He always will be. For him there was nothing

"Maybe the greatest athlete in Michigan history."

"Sometimes the natives get a little restless."

"Nice car, but Bennie never took it too far out of Ann Arbor. That was home and he loved it."

greater in life than wearing the Michigan uniform or leading young men to Michigan glory."

Oosterbaan had the ability to make everyone feel he was the neighbor next door. He was a players' coach. He had an ability to make everyone feel at ease. His players called him "Bennie" or "Coach." He was never a shouter, but his message was always clear.

"He had that look," said Kramer who was a two-time All-American under Oosterbaan. "He looked at everyone but he gave you the feeling he was looking squarely at you."

His theme never wavered.

"He spoke of the Michigan tradition," Kramer said. "He spoke of pride. He always

said that everyone at Michigan is family. Not just the team he was coaching but everyone who had played before us. They were all looking at us and were actually part of us. He was extremely sincere because he loved Michigan that much."

Oosterbaan became the first assistant under Fritz Crisler and took over the head job in 1948. Oosterbaan was a genius on offense and is credited with masterminding the plays for the celebrated "Mad Magicians."

In his first season, Oosterbaan guided Michigan to a 9-0 record and a national championship. For his efforts he was named National Coach of the Year.

As a player, Oosterbaan had few peers. As

an end, he became the first of only two Michigan players to win All-American honors three times (1925-1927). His number 47 was retired.

He was named All-American twice in basketball. He was an All-Big Ten baseball player and finished his career with nine varsity letters. He refused professional baseball and football offers to remain as a coach at his beloved Michigan.

"There was nothing phony about Bennie," Kramer said. "He believed in Michigan and wasn't afraid to say so. He believed very strongly that all of us are Michigan. And we must live up to the standards that are expected of us."

"From his helicopter, Bennie Oosterbaan had a pretty good view of spring practice."

"Friedman was the 'other' Benny and he was pretty good. He was the guy throwing all those passes to Oosterbaan."

OF MUTUAL RESPECT

Their outward appearances are practically polar.

They're as diverse as a game-ending Hail Mary touchdown pass and a heart-breaking interception.

Bo is charismatic and fearlessly wears each emotion openly. Lloyd Carr features his own brand of charisma. Inherently more reserved, Carr's strength lies in the subtlety of his commitment to excellence.

Beneath the obvious personality differences, however, the passion for Michigan Football and reverence for coaching with integrity are identical in the Ol' Coach and his successor.

Their paths to what each consider "the best job in college football" were as different as their personality strengths. Yet each highly regards the other for the virtues both share. Compare a candid conversation with both.

From the Ol' Coach

Talking about Lloyd Carr you must begin with honesty. I never met another coach as honest as Lloyd.

NEVER!

If a man is not completely honest, it's impossible to be truly successful regardless what he does. That's especially true with coaching young men in college.

"Not just the Rose Bowl champions...the National Champions!"

Lloyd's honesty carries a powerful message. It tells all of his players, all of his assistants, all of the trainers and everyone connected to the program that if he says something, they can count on it. One-hundred percent of the time!

Not just in good times. That's the easy part. But also when times get tough. That makes so much difference when a person can rely on a man whose word is his bond.

When Lloyd says there's no other coaching job in the world that could take him away from Michigan, he means it. The players, the recruits, the staff, the administration don't have to worry that he's out looking for another job. That's a tremendous asset for the program. And his program is in EXCELLENT shape.

If you want to get a measure of a coach, take a look at the players he brings into the program.

I tried to make as few mistakes as possible evaluating character when I recruited because – I guarantee you – those mistakes will come back to haunt you. It's impossible to be perfect with your evaluations. You can't have a hundred guys without a couple turning out to be not what you expected.

But then you get rid of them. And that's exactly what Lloyd does.

Lloyd places so much emphasis on the quality of a kid's character. He has the ability to relate to young people. He's good at that because he tells them the truth. That makes him a good recruiter.

Sometimes being honest can cost you a few recruits. That's better than compromising your principles by making promises you know you can't keep.

Character is a major ingredient of every class Lloyd's recruited. He cares about the kids who come here. He's concerned that the kids who do commit to Michigan are the kind of kids who appreciate what the Michigan tradition is all about.

It's not a "me" program. It's all about the TEAM!

Some people misread Lloyd. He's a tough disciplinarian. His mild manner belies his toughness to make a decision and stand by it.

Lloyd Carr does not lack confidence. He has never looked at me as being in his way because I keep an office in the football building. As a matter of fact, I think he enjoys it.

We like each other. We kid each other. We respect each other. Once in a while we have some confidential talks on important matters. But he's certainly not afraid to make every major decision on his own.

If I thought for one minute – ONE MINUTE – that he would be better off without me here, I'd be history. I simply enjoy being around. There's nothing more fun than being around football coaches and a program like the University of Michigan.

As I reflect on my career and the condition of today's Michigan Football program I feel very gratified. That's important to me.

There's no better feeling in the world.

About the Ol' Coach

Sir Isaac Newton once made a statement that, in my opinion, puts success into perspective. He said: "If I have seen further than most men it is because I have been able to stand at the shoulder of giants."

Bo Schembechler is one of the truly great coaches in the history of the game — a remarkable man who left the legacy of a giant.

His record speaks for itself — the winningest coach in the history of the winningest program. And don't forget, he retired early. He was a great organizer, a stickler for detail and without peer as a motivator. His teams seldom beat themselves and that was due to the discipline that was a trademark of his teams. No one possessed a

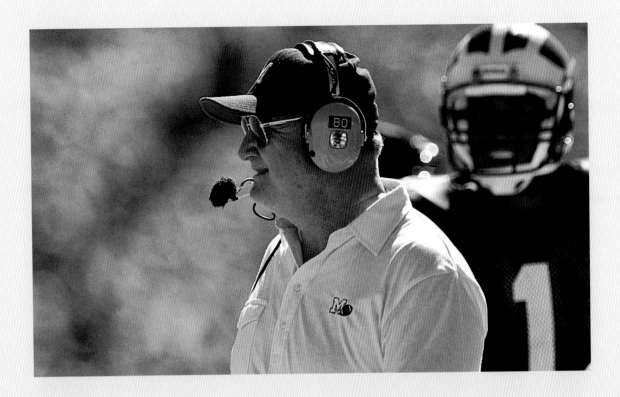

greater will to win and no one outworked him. Stubborn? Absolutely!!! Most of the great ones are.

He knew exactly how he was going to try to win and he was not influenced by those who criticized his ways. And yet, when change was necessary, he was flexible enough to change.

But Bo is much more than a great football coach. He is a man who is principled, who would not compromise his values to win. He won big, but he won within the rules and that is why he is as well respected by his peers as anyone who has coached the game.

One of the happiest days of my coaching career was March 12, 1980, the day Bo hired me as an assistant coach. I found him to be tough, demanding and intimidating. I also found him to be fair, generous and loyal.

He was great fun to be around and the thing I miss most since he left are his staff meetings. He loved a good argument, particularly one centered on politics. He had definite opinions on the way the country should be run. Anyone who had the temerity to disagree with him was immediately labeled a "soft, do good liberal." But that's another story.

Was Bo the greatest coach ever at Michigan? I have read most of what has been written about Coach Yost and Coach Crisler and I have heard a lot of stories from men who knew them and played or coached for them. They are men of legendary status and the question cannot be definitively answered because each man coached in a much different era. I never saw the Yost or Crisler teams, and therefore, my opinion is biased. I had the great fortune to know Bo, to coach for him and to be great friends with him.

Who was Michigan's greatest coach? Bo Schembechler. That's just one man's opinion.

"Give me a minute and I'll think of something."

"Gary Moeller was a tremendously innovative offensive coach and as hard working a coach as I've seen."

A STRONG TRADITION

"When it comes to strength and conditioning, Mike Gittleson is the best."

Bo Schembechler started a tradition in 1978 that is paying greater dividends today than anyone may have expected.

He created a position and hired a coach. Not just any coach. He hired Mike Gittleson to run the strength and conditioning program.

"We are truly blessed to have Mike," Bo said. "He's one of the most important persons in the program because the strength coach is the only one that can coach the players all year long."

Obviously, that calls for a special type of person. And without doubt, Gittleson is, indeed, quite that person.

"Mike has a tremendous knowledge of the human body and knows how to develop it for a tough combat game like football," Bo explained. "He's a Vietnam War vet. He's extremely well read. He knows how to get into the mind of each individual he works with. He's a tremendous motivator."

Not surprisingly, Gittleson learned so many

"Tom Dixon knows that a center has to be tough."

of his coaching techniques from the master himself.

"Coach Schembechler is beautiful," Gittleson said. "He has what's called tremendous 'fellowship with humanity.' He has a deep identification with people. He gives you a feeling that you're important. He always has time for his fellow man. He listens. That's a beautiful quality. He may not agree with what you're saying, but he always listens."

There was no such thing as a strength and conditioning coach before Gittleson's arrival. Those duties were shared by assistant coaches. In today's game, weight training and conditioning are as critical to a successful program as quality special teams.

"Because of the limit on scholarships," Bo explained, "teams can't go out and hit every day in practice like we used to. No coach can run the risk of losing key players to injury. Therefore, players have to be made stronger and tougher in the weight room. How they respond to such training often is reflected in the way they perform on the field. And Mike Gittleson makes them respond."

Gittleson's approach to players is only a superficial paradox.

"I coach them all the same, but different," he said.

He devotes the same amount of time and energy to each player. But his means of motivation differ according to personality.

"Believe me when I tell you," Bo explained. "Mike knows when to pump a kid up and when to challenge him. He spends as much time with a walk-on as he does with one of the highly recruited kids. He knows how to motivate."

Gittleson was wise enough to embrace Bo's lessons.

"When I came into the program, I figured the players were lifting weights and running,"

"Curtis Greer kind of reminds me of myself when I work out."

Gittleson said. "After a while, I realized these kids weren't coming to Michigan to become runners and weightlifters. They came here to play football. So there was going to be a little bit of a struggle to get the excellence that you knew was inside of these young men.

"I had a great concern about these athletes so I went to Coach Schembechler about a few of those I couldn't get to participate the way I wanted.

"I sat down with the coach and listed all my problems. He looked at me and said something I'll never forget. 'Mike, anyone can coach the ones who are willing. Your job is to coach the ones who aren't.'"

Today such issues rarely exist. Strength and conditioning have become essential to the sport.

"Kids come out of high school much better prepared," Gittleson said. "They realize this is an integral part of athleticism. Everyone jumps on board. It's just another part of the sport."

Gittleson's Michigan journey – which has led to similar positions on every major college staff – followed some strange turns.

After serving in the military, Gittleson earned degrees from the University of New Hampshire (1975) and Plymouth State College (1977) where he graduated summa cum laude with a 3.9 grade point average. He lettered in football, track and wrestling. He won the state weightlifting championship.

He was at Michigan on a scholarship working toward his master's degree in exercise science when a professor introduced him to Bo in 1978.

"I was training for the national collegiate power lifting championship and hurt myself," Gittleson recalled. "I wanted to use a machine in the weight room. Bo was looking for someone to work with his team. I told him I would if I could use the facilities. One thing led to another."

And it certainly paid off for Gittleson and the university.

"How about some of Gittleson's finest, ladies?"

"I had already played sports so I was not enamored with Michigan football," Gittleson said. "But there was something special about Bo. And I was enamored with the university.

"Strength and conditioning is like every aspect of our program. I charge myself with giving every player a special experience. If a young man elects to play football for the University of Michigan, he does so because he knows it's special. If a student goes to the school of engineering here he expects it to be special. It's the university.

"When I came here in kinesiology I expected a lot. And I got it. I hold this university in such high regard I believe this program should give a kid what he expects. I want every parent who drops their kid off here to feel good about it because they're entrusting their sons to the Michigan football program."

And Gittleson refuses to let that tradition down.

FROM MY OWN PLAY BOOK

The 54-55 Draw was one of the favorite plays I kept in my play book.

Except for short yardage or goal line downs, I called this play on any down anywhere on the field. The beauty of this play was that you could pass or run the draw off the same formation. The draw play looked like a play action pass because the protection looked nearly the same. It was hard for the defense to distinguish whether their linebackers should be dropping back to defend the pass or step up to stop the draw.

We showed the play early in the game to set up the defense. We ran it on first, second or third down.

And it was very effective.

<u>54-55 DRAW</u>

129

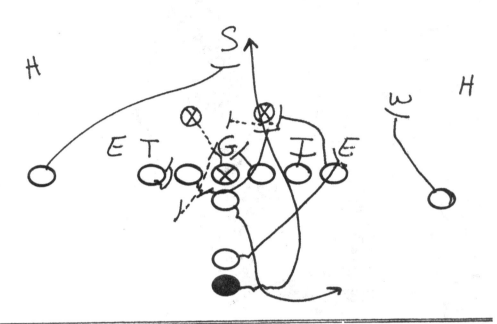

<u>COACHING POINTS</u>: 1) Good splits 2) Release and block of TE
3) Timing and read of TB and BSG 4) Seal of BS.

<u>CALLS</u>: 4

<u>BLOCKING RULES</u>:

FSWR: Run crack course and block inside deep defender.

FSTE: Release inside for FS-BSLB.

FST: Zoom block down lineman on, inside.

FSG: Odd: drive inside.
Even: fold unless tackle covered, then take #1.

C: Odd: backside lead #0 to EOL.
Even: block BS #1.

BSG: Set and then pull to block first LB FS. (Even: MLB eagle: FSLB).

BST: Set and take BS #2.

BSE: Release inside for BS LB.

BSWR: Crossfield and block middle 1/3.

FB: Block the call.

TB: Ball.

QB: Give ball to TB. Fake 54-55 pass.

"It was a privilege for me just standing with these men (left to right) Harry Kipke, Fritz Crisler, Bennie Oosterbaan, Bump Elliott, and myself."

"That's the coach talking and everybody better listen."

"These guys go all the way back to 1940. Any coach would take this backfield today. That's (from the left) Forest Evashevski, Norm Call, Bob Westfall and the great Tom Harmon. Beautiful!"

"That's Fielding H. Yost and his team on a trolley ride at the 1902 Rose Bowl. Incidentally, in the game, Michigan nipped Stanford, 49-0."

"Does anybody recognize the crafty left-hander? Here comes the heat."

"A coach in the making. That's Harry Kipke punting a ball for Coach Yost. How about that form?"

"January 1, 1981 — my first Rose Bowl victory. We closed out the season with 22 consecutive quarters without allowing a touchdown against us. When we finished, we were the best team in the nation."

SPECIAL SATURDAYS THEN AND NOW

"There is no finer setting anywhere in the United States of America than Ann Arbor, Michigan on a football Saturday," claims Bo Schembechler.

"None! The tailgate parties, the color, the sounds, the feelings, the tradition. Now that I see the whole spectacle, it's more enormous than I realized when I was down on the field."

Bo watches all games from his booth in the pressbox. And the passion remains.

"The only difference is now I can't grab any player by the collar and tell him what to do," Bo cracked.

Here's a snapshot of football weekends, then and now.

THE OL' COACH THEN ON A MICHIGAN FOOTBALL WEEKEND

Friday

• After classes, the team convened for meetings and a "walk through" of Saturday's game plan. Players ran through a series of plays before three buses arrived to transport them to the Campus Inn Hotel for the night.

"Shirts, ties and sportcoats were mandatory," Bo emphasized. "We looked like a real team."

• The team headed to the upper two floors – offense on top and defense right below.

There was a team dinner of steaks and pasta in a private dining room.

"We needed the men strong and ready," Bo said.

• Players then changed into sweats for a movie in a private room. "I picked the movie," Bo said. "I loved Clint Eastwood westerns."

• Then it was back to the rooms for cookies and hot chocolate. Two players to a room and Bo visited each one to personally turn out the lights at around 9:30.

"I'd ask them if they were ready and things like that," Bo said. "Then I'd go back to my room and watch more films of our opponent."

Saturday

• Around 7 a.m., a walk around the block was followed by chapel service and a Mass.

"Sometimes after Mass, the Catholic players would drift into the chapel service," Bo said. "They were getting extra prepared."

• After a pregame meal, players were treated to a talk from Bo. "This was my main speech," Bo said.

"Then they were prepared to go out and hit."

• In shirt, tie and sportcoat, the team

departed on three buses, with police escort, to the stadium ready for battle. "Once they got into uniform, we sat them all down in chairs," Bo explained. "Offense on one side of the room and defense on the other. All we did was go over a few last minute details. There was no need for another speech. I already had done that at the hotel. We'd talk again at halftime. If you noticed, we always played better in the second half. We came out stronger and took advantage of the things we saw."

- At game time, players were ready to charge onto the field. "There's no other feeling in the world like running out of that tunnel," Bo said. "Absolutely none!"

THE OL' COACH NOW

Friday

- Friday nights are calmer now. Bo spends them at home with Cathy. Sometimes there are dinners at a restaurant with out-of-town guests.

  "For certain games I get a little nervous on Friday because all I can do is worry," Bo said.

Saturday

- Around 10 a.m., Bo and Cathy arrive at the stadium. As they walk from the gate to the pressbox elevator, fans start to buzz: "Hey Bo, how you doing?...How we going to do today?"

  "I love the fans," Bo said. "Michigan fans are the greatest. But I try to walk fast. If you stop for a few autographs you get caught in a crowd. I need to get up to the booth and prepare for the game."

- Around 11 a.m., Bo is in his booth studying the opponent's depth chart and reviewing its media guide which he already had perused all week.

"I like to study the opposing personnel... know who's strong and who's weak," Bo said. "In a third and one I know which player to attack. I study all the books. I watch all the games on TV and I review the tapes. So when I sit up there before a game I watch them warm up. I can tell when they line up what play a team is going to run. I can't do anything about it, but I like to be prepared."

- Around noon, Bo studies the Michigan team as it charges from the tunnel and players leap to touch the Michigan banner.

  "I still watch the way they come out," Bo said. "I can tell if it's a false enthusiasm or the real thing. I could tell when I was coaching and I can tell now. The only difference is when I was coaching I could grab a player and impress upon him that he better get with it. All I can do now is worry."

- Some time during the first half - at least by the second - Bo stands up to question an official's call.

  "I've never thrown anything in my booth, but I have expressed my displeasure," Bo cracked.

- Shortly after 4 p.m., Bo is back at home. Following a Michigan victory, there is no sweeter Saturday evening.

  "I get back and immediately turn on the TV," Bo said. "I watch all the games, even the late ones from the west coast. The worst thing for me is watching one of our road games on TV. Between plays you can't study the sidelines. You can't read the body language. It's hard to get a real feel for what's unfolding. But, of course, I have to watch."

So while so much has changed, so much has remained the same. For Bo, the passion doesn't die.

BETTER THAN THE HATFIELDS & MᶜCOYS

Woody...you're warming up on the wrong side of the field.

— Bo Schembechler

T here is NO greater rivalry in intercollegiate football than the one we have with Michigan and Ohio State.

NONE!

There are some other great ones around the country. Every one of them is good for the sport and good for their schools.

But the Michigan/Ohio State rivalry is special. You can line up all the others and they still wind up as bridesmaids.

It doesn't matter what part of the country you talk about. This one is the best.

These two teams have played each other every year since 1918. And with the exception of 1942, it's been the last regular game of the season since 1935.

No other game annually has as much riding on it.

There's the conference championship. There's normally a Rose Bowl bid involved. And in some way, the national rankings always get a shake-up after this game.

On top of it all, it seems like the students at these two schools simply don't like each other.

When we coached against each other, the media made a big thing out of the "Woody/Bo Wars." I suppose all the hype was good for the game. But no one needs any extra motivation for this one. Players on both sides of the field don't worry about who's coaching on the other sideline.

But I have to admit...those battles were fun.

We were right here in Ann Arbor for the first one. Woody had his team on the field for practice when I was taking mine down the tunnel. I looked out and

"Never go on that field down there without adequate protection."

saw Ohio State warming up on our side of the field.

I knew it was Woody. He already had coached a lot of games here. He knew where he was supposed to be. He was testing me. Now he's got my players watching to see what I would do.

I walked straight to him. Very calm. Very deliberate.

"Woody...you're warming up on the wrong side of the field," I said.

"You should be down at the other end."

He looked back. Very calm. Very deliberate.

"O.K.," he said. "We'll go down to that end. Come on men. Let's go."

My guys liked that. They knew this is our house and we set the rules.

That's the way he was, though. He'd always play little psychological games.

What a lot of people don't know is that Woody and I rarely talked to each other. We both respected each other. I admired him very much. But there was no cause for a lot of talking.

When all of the coaches got together at the Big Ten meetings in July we'd talk. That was it. In those 10 years we coached against each other, I never dialed the phone to call him and he never dialed the phone to talk to me.

That's just the way it was.

Before the games when we played, he'd tell one of my assistants, "You tell Coach Schembechler I'm ready to meet him at the 50."

My assistant would tell me and I'd go over to shake his hand. NEVER did I go over to his side of the 50. And NEVER did he step over to my side.

"Hi, Woody, how're you doing?" I'd ask him. "How's Anne?"

He'd say the same thing to me. That was it till the next year.

I loved the guy. I played for him. I coached for him. But that's just the way we always handled the situation.

I loved those games. We always knew what they were going to do and they knew what we were going to do. We both had each other's moves down cold.

"In 1997, Glen Steele let that Buckeye quarterback know what this game is all about. If it looks rough, you should hear how it sounds down there."

"When it is over, both sides know they've played a great game."

Captain Mike Mallory was the first of three of Coach Bill Mallory's sons to play for Michigan.

One thing everybody knew for sure was there was going to be some good old-fashioned, up close, hard-hitting football. I mean HARD-HITTING. It was punishing. It was real football.

When those two teams walked off that field after each one of those games, win or lose, both squads knew they had been in a football game.

That's what really made those games special. It still does. Those games are played with more intensity and more guts than anything you could make up for a Hollywood movie.

We did something in practice just for that game all year long. We made little adjustments that we saved just for them. They did the same thing for us.

It always got down to outblocking and outtackling the other guy and not making any mistakes. That's still the way it is today.

Woody and I tangled 10 times. Michigan finished on top, 5-4-1. That's pretty good against a school with the tradition of Ohio State. It shows just how tough this rivalry always has been. I'm proud of that.

After Woody retired, he called me one day during the season.

"Bo, this is Woody," he said. "I've got to give a speech up there."

"Good," I said. "Come out to practice."

When he arrived, I called my men together.

"Men, I want you to meet our old nemesis," I said. "This is the great Woody Hayes."

He talked to my men. It was a great scene.

This rivalry will outlive all of us. In college football, there is none better.

"Looks like Michigan just pulled off another good one."

"BO, YOU'LL NEVER WIN A BIGGER GAME."

— Woody

In the middle of the Vietnam War...nation-wide civil unrest...various student protests...and a generally changing American society, Bo arrived at Michigan to change the face of Wolverine Football.

He didn't exactly tiptoe up U.S. 23 from Ohio. He more or less bulldozed through anything that stood in his way.

"Bo arrived in Ann Arbor the same way General Patton arrived in Europe," Dan

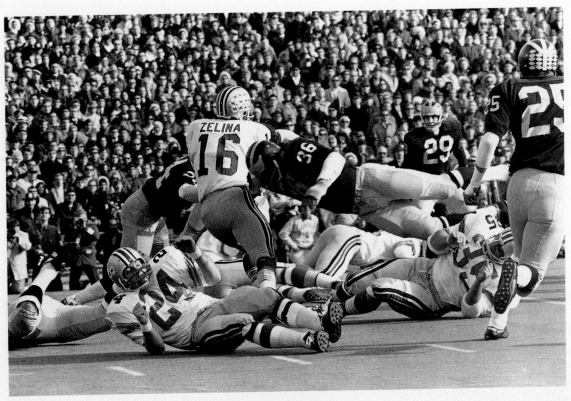

"My guys were simply not impressed by the Ohio State ranking."

Dierdorf said. "He's not exactly an inconspicuous person."

His arrival signaled the start of the modern era of Michigan Football.

"There's no question in my mind," Dierdorf said. "That 1969 season, and particularly the victory over Ohio State, took a program that had been O.K. since the late 1940s and vaulted it into something exceptional which hasn't stopped to this day."

Bo's program was simple. It was built on discipline, dedication, sweat, and blood. During spring practice of 1969, a lot of returning players did not survive the blitz.

"You have to recognize the climate of those times," said Jim Brandstatter, who is proud he stuck it out. "It was a very political era and the University was sort of the Berkeley of the Midwest."

Bo established a program of commitment

"Look at that scoreboard!"

that many felt more resembled Marine Corps training than a football camp.

"We took pride in the fact that there might have been a Marine brigade somewhere in the

"One of those special moments that will always live in my heart."

world better than us, but no one was in better shape," said Fritz Seyferth.

"There's a challenge and a testing of the mettle that we all have to go through in our lives. He tested ours. I promise you those who stayed acquired a whole different opinion of themselves and others and what can be accomplished with a commitment."

Many were unable to make that commitment. Spring practice started with about 125 players. By week's end, it had dwindled to about 85.

Even some who stayed at times questioned Bo's relentless drive.

"I was one of them," Dierdorf said. "But I was 19-years-old and what the heck did I know? Obviously, Bo was right and I was wrong."

Before practice began, Bo and his staff made their own commitment. Bo had that now-famous "Those Who Stay Will Be Champions" sign hung in the locker room.

"During the week, one of the guys who quit took a Magic Marker and wrote under it, 'those who don't will be doctors and lawyers and other important people,'" Brandstatter said.

"But Bo made us all better men. There was never a time when we were physically or mentally stronger. I'll always be grateful for the experience."

In spite of an army of skeptics, Bo never doubted his program would work.

"According to the people who were here when I came, there was no way I could be successful," Bo said. "They said these methods would not work at Michigan. The University is a very liberal campus and kids simply would not accept that kind of discipline.

"They found out that if you present something that is good...if you are honest...and everyone wants to be successful...and this is

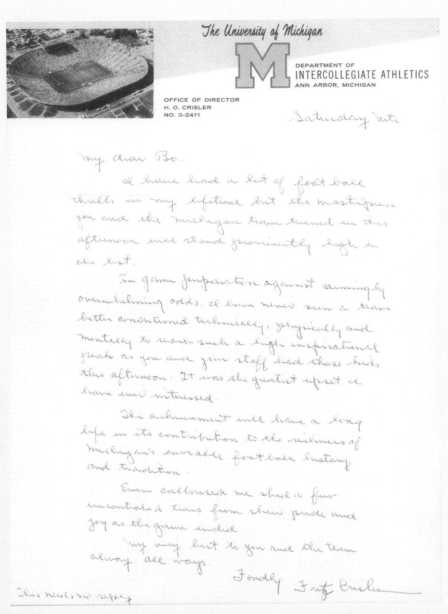

The University of Michigan

M DEPARTMENT OF
INTERCOLLEGIATE ATHLETICS
ANN ARBOR, MICHIGAN

OFFICE OF DIRECTOR
H. O. CRISLER
NO. 3-2411

Saturday nite

My dear Bo.

I have had a lot of foot ball thrills in my lifetime but the masterpiece you and the Michigan team turned in this afternoon will stand prominently high in the list.

In game preparation against seemingly overwhelming odds, I have never seen a team better conditioned technically, physically and mentally to work such a high inspirational peak as you and your staff had those kids this afternoon. It was the greatest upset I have ever witnessed.

The achievement will have a long life in its contribution to the richness of Michigan's enviable foot ball history and tradition.

Even calloused me shed a few uncontrolled tears from sheer pride and joy as the game ended

My very best to you and the team always all ways.

Fondly Fritz Crisler

This needs no reply

"Fritz Crisler was lying ill in the hospital when he wrote me this letter after the 1969 win over Ohio State. When I read it I cried. It hangs on my wall at home."

the best way to achieve it...then they will accept it. They actually crave discipline if it's for the right reasons."

And so the modern era of Michigan Football was born.

"From the day Bo was carried off the field after we beat Ohio State in 1969, things have never been quite the same at the stadium or wherever Michigan goes," Dierdorf said. "We had beaten what many people considered to be the best college team ever assembled. We were perceived differently. And that's still true today."

Those who stay do, in fact, become champions.

GET IT RIGHT

Jim Brandstatter now laughs affectionately over the beginning of his lifelong friendship with Bo Schembechler.

At Tuesday's practice after Michigan suffered a blocked punt in a game the previous Saturday, the demonstration team blocked one on the varsity. Bo already had promised the demo team that anyone who blocked a punt would get a milk shake.

That wasn't quite what Brandstatter received.

"As soon as it happened, Bo came charging 40 yards down the field screaming," Brandstatter now recalls with a smile. "He was screaming: 'Brandstatter, you leave the field. You're the worst tackle in the history of intercollegiate football.'"

Brandstatter was stunned. He was moved to tears, thinking his Michigan football career was over in just his sophomore year. Actually, the defender had run over the player lined up next to him. One of the assistant coaches talked to Bo and told Brandstatter to stay.

On Friday, Bo approached Brandstatter.

"You don't think that was your fault, do you?" Bo asked.

"Coach, I know it wasn't my fault," Brandstatter answered.

"Well...you moved your feet too far apart anyway," Bo responded.

Now both teacher and student laugh about the incident. Both treasure their friendship of almost 35 years.

It wasn't until after he completed his Michigan football career in 1971 that Brandstatter fully appreciated Bo's design of developing character in young men.

"When you were a sophomore, all he tried to do was to push you," Brandstatter said. "He wanted you to become the best disciplined athlete and person you could possibly be. It was rough, but that's the only way he knew how to do it. And it worked.

"When you were a junior, you sort of understood what he was doing. By the time you became a senior, you realized your role of leadership. You then became a conduit to continue the tradition of Michigan Football. It's after you graduate, though, when you totally appreciate what Bo and Michigan Football has meant to your life. I could never thank either one of

"Look at Jimmy's form. He's got a great career in broadcasting ahead of him."

them enough for what they mean to me."

Brandstatter played offensive tackle for the Wolverines from 1969-1971. Today he is a popular Detroit area radio and television football analyst for both the University of Michigan and the Detroit Lions.

He proudly states that his years at Michigan were "absolutely the best time of my life."

"It's hard to express, but the Michigan Football tradition is different than at other schools," he said.

"Uniforms change, year in and year out. Not at Michigan. Look at pictures of Tom Harmon and he's wearing that winged helmet. So is Ron Kramer. His No. 87 is retired. When he visits the program, those kids realize the importance of the past on the present and their responsibility to it.

"It's sort of like the attitude the Marines have for their uniform. They show tremendous respect for that uniform. It's the same at Michigan. When a young man puts on that maize and blue and that winged helmet, he's well aware of all the great ones who have gone before him. He knows he must perform to an expected level of excellence."

Brandstatter's admiration for Bo mirrors his respect for the Michigan Football tradition.

"He's honest," he said. "He's straightforward. He doesn't come in the side door. He's got the highest ethical standards and he's not afraid to let you know what they are.

"Most important is that he genuinely cares for people. He wants all young men who attend the University of Michigan to become the best football players they can possibly be. But he wants them to do it the right way. He wants them to do it with character."

Brandstatter marvels at Bo's unassuming humility.

"He truly is a legend," Brandstatter said. "But he just wants to be one of the guys. He never thinks what he accomplished is any great thing. He's a coach and he feels teaching and coaching is an admirable profession. That humility is not fake. He truly is the greatest living symbol of what the University of Michigan Football tradition is all about."

STILL AN "M" MAN

During the football off-seasons when he attended Michigan, Dan Dierdorf used to sit alone in the stadium.

"I love the place," he said. "When I was a freshman we couldn't play varsity. So I'd go over to the stadium and dream about how it would feel to come charging out of that tunnel for a game."

Over the next three seasons, he certainly got his chance. From 1968 through 1970, Dierdorf was one of the most feared offensive tackles in the country.

He was a consensus All-American in 1970. He later starred for the St. Louis Cardinals and was a 1996 inductee into the National Football League Hall of Fame. He is a long-time network broadcaster for NFL telecasts.

"There's no way to describe just how big that stadium is when you come out of that tunnel," he said. "In the tunnel, you can't see

"He was the best offensive lineman I ever had."

anything. When you come out, it's like a snap-shot. One minute you're in darkness and the next minute you're in the middle of the whole deal.

"It can take your breath away. You wouldn't want to put an EKG on the players in that tunnel. I'm sure there are a few skipped heartbeats. The resting pulse is probably 150. It's stressful, but it's tremendous."

Even after his Hall of Fame professional career and notoriety from being part of Monday Night Football, Dierdorf holds his college days at Michigan as one of the most precious parts of his life.

"There are so many images and friend-ships," he said. "Every time I see them, men-tally I revert to being nineteen and twenty years old. I even think the way I did then. I'm assuming that will last till the day I die."

The tradition of Michigan Football still lives within Dierdorf.

"You can't be in Ann Arbor and participate in the football program without being aware of, and also honor bound to its tradition," he said. "It might sound hokey, but that tradi-tion really is passed from class to class. It's a fiber that connects all of us.

"The thing that really impresses me is not only the length of its success, but also that it is a clean, above board and honorable pro-gram. All of us who have participated in the Michigan program realize there's a lot more to it than simply the wins in the record book."

Dierdorf was recruited to Michigan by Bump Elliott. He played his last two years under Bo Schembechler.

"I had the rare opportunity to be coached by one of the most remarkable personalities I've ever been around," Dierdorf said. "All of us who played for Bo were completely domi-nated by his will and personality. Most people are never in direct contact with someone who has that type of overwhelming personality.

"It's affected all of us. How often does it happen that you are in the circle of someone who is larger than life? It takes an exceptional man to drive 90 people as straight and as narrow as he drove us just on the strength of his will and sheer presence. We won because we were afraid to lose."

Dierdorf confirms that Bo always had a sense of humor as keen as his desire to win.

"That was one of his best qualities," Dierdorf said. "As demanding as he was, he could make the entire team laugh instantly. There were times we would just burst out laughing at something he said or did.

"One minute he'd be growling. And in the next breath he might say the guy who makes a great play will get a milk shake. We were always guessing at what was coming. That was his strong suit. I've never met anyone like him and I mean that in a most complimentary way. I'd do anything for the man."

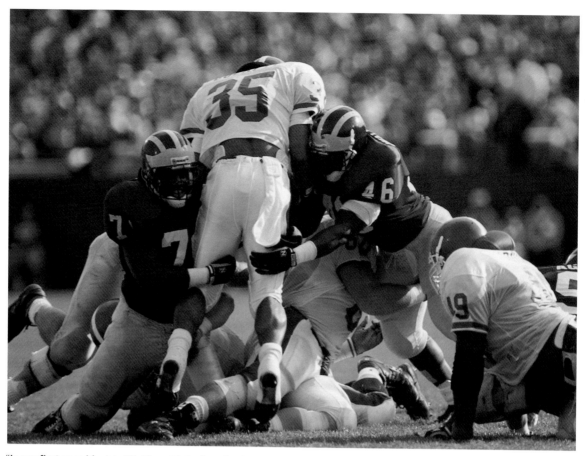

"In my first year I lost to Michigan State. I realized right then, I can't let this happen too often."

"That's Stan Edwards leaving white shirted Spartans behind."

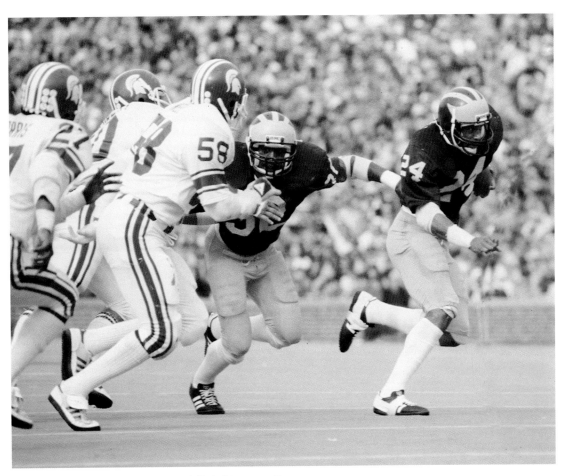

"Butch Woolfolk played hard — especially in big games."

"Coach Yost put on a Spartan blanket, but I bet he didn't wear it during the game."

"Sometimes the students get a little excited after big games."

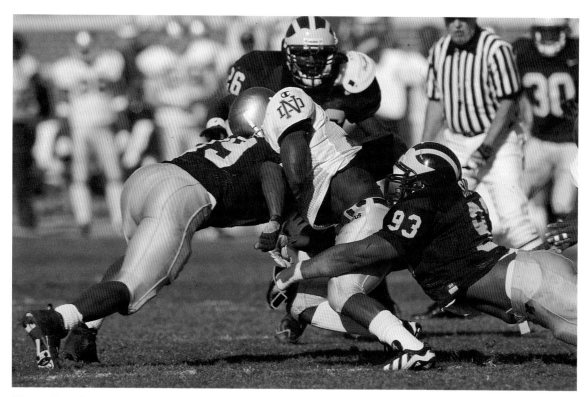

"No, no Notre Dame."

"Notre Dame is, by far, the most intense nonconference rivalry."

"Not against Michigan, you don't."

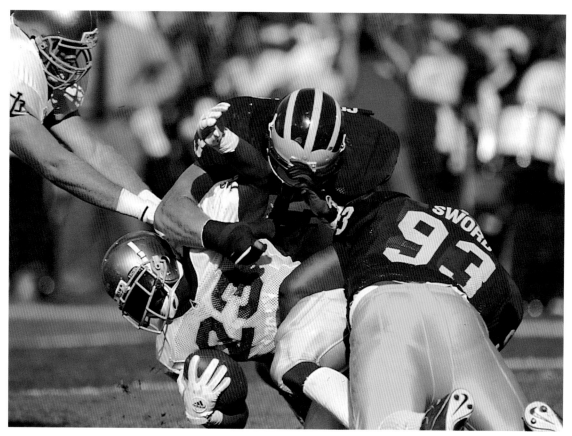

"A beautiful sight — a gold helmet down and that magnificent striped one on top."

"We'll put an end to this nonsense real quick."

"Yes, we have some of those too."

"The Paul Bunyan Trophy was initiated by Governor G. Mennen Williams in 1953 and goes to the winner of the Michigan-Michigan State game. It looks nice in Ann Arbor."

THE REAL THING

The real Little Brown Jug is locked in a wooden box and carefully stored in the equipment room in Schembechler Hall.

Equipment Manager Jon Falk is responsible for its security. He brings it out on the day of the Michigan-Minnesota game and carries it to the field where one of his assistants guards it on the sidelines.

The winner of the game keeps the treasured jug until the two teams meet the following year. For more than the last half century, the Little Brown Jug has found a home in Ann Arbor. Going into the 2003 season, Michigan has beaten Minnesota in 47 of its last 58 meetings, including 31 of the last 33 and 14 in a row.

The battle for the Little Brown Jug literally is the granddaddy of all intercollegiate football trophy games. There are 57 such games played annually around the country. All owe their creation to this traditional rivalry.

It started back in 1903 in Minnesota. Michigan Coach Fielding Yost doubted that his rival would supply pure water to the Michigan bench. He ordered one of his staff to purchase a jug to avoid any problem.

After Minnesota scored late for a 6-6 tie, pandemonium broke out in the stands. The game was called with time left on the clock. In their haste to leave, Michigan left the jug on the field. It was discovered by Minnesota equipment manager Oscar Munson who gave it to his athletic director. On the jug, the Gophers painted: "Michigan Jug – Captured by Oscar, October 31, 1903," and the score "Minnesota 6, Michigan 6."

When Yost sent a letter requesting the jug's return, the Minnesota athletic director wrote back, "If you want it, you'll have to come up and win it."

And over the years, Michigan certainly has.

The two teams did not meet again until 1909 when Michigan won, 15-6.

The jug disappeared from Michigan's trophy case in 1930 and was missing until 1934. Before the actual jug was found behind a clump of bushes by a gas station attendant in Ann Arbor, a replica stood in the trophy case. The authenticity of the original was confirmed by a flaw that could not have been duplicated.

Now the jug has truly found a home. And it truly is the real thing.

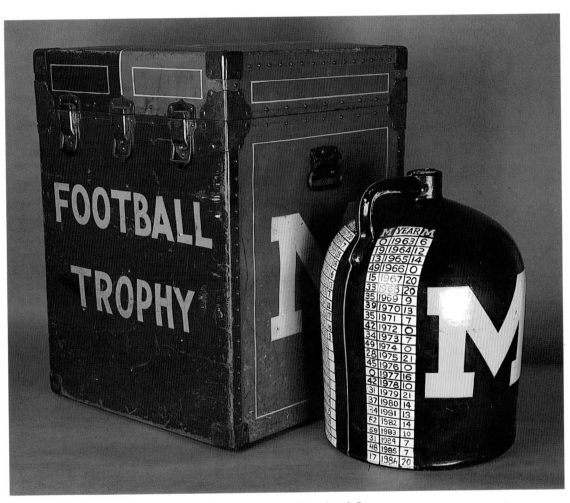

"I never realized how important the Little Brown Jug was until we lost it."

ROSES IN THE SNOW

It snowed the day after Thanksgiving in 1950. On the next day in Columbus, a blizzard struck so fiercely that it was almost impossible to see the field.

Nature nudged its way into creating a chunk of college football folklore with the "Snow Bowl" in Columbus.

There were 50,503 fans caked in icicles as the Wolverines and Buckeyes battled in conditions better suited for polar bears. Nearly a half-century later, the game still is relived in wonder, even by those who were born long after the historical event.

"We bussed to Toledo before taking the train to Columbus," said Michigan fullback Don Dufek. "When we got there, the train parked on a rail. We looked out the windows and saw all these people slipping and sliding and falling down."

Dufek still smiles when recalling the scene.

"All the coaches walked down the aisle and yelled 'pull your shades down,'" he said. "I guess they didn't want us to see how bad the conditions were."

But the game was played. And it still sparkles brightly in the treasure chest of college football memories.

Despite heroic efforts to keep the field clean by sweeping between plays, snow and ice made it impossible for either team to move the ball. Not only couldn't they move it, they had trouble merely seeing the yard lines.

The teams combined on a staggering 45 punts. Michigan could not make a first down. Ohio State eked out two.

But Michigan persisted. After falling behind by a field goal that, at the time, must have looked as secure as Fort Knox, Michigan rallied to block two punts – one for a safety and another for a touchdown.

"Two guys who really deserve a lot of credit were Chuck Ortmann and Carl Kreager," Dufek said. "Ortmann did a great job of punting all day. Kreager was the center. Despite the conditions, he did not make one bad snap."

And the magic went beyond Columbus. While Michigan doggedly defeated both Ohio State and Mother Nature, in Evanston, Northwestern upset Illinois to vault the Wolverines into the Rose Bowl.

Pitted against undefeated California, Michigan rallied with a pair of fourth quarter touchdowns to upset the 4th-ranked Golden Bears, 14-6. It was Dufek who scored both Michigan touchdowns and was named the game's Most Valuable Player.

"It sounds poetic," he said, "but I guess there really were roses in that snow at Columbus."

And forever that miserable snow and ice and beautiful roses will remain a piece of Michigan tradition.

MOMSEN—M.

"That's Tony Momsen recovering a fumble for the only touchdown in the 1950 'Snow Bowl'. Games like that separate the men from the boys."

OHIO STATE COACHING STAFF

Front row, left to right: Gene Fekete, junior varsity coach; Bo Schembechler, assistant junior varsity coach; Bill Arnsparger, tackle coach; Bill Hess, guard coach. Back row: Doyt Perry, backfield coach; Harry Strobel, defensive line coach; W. W. (Woody) Hayes, head coach. Esco Sarkkinen, end coach; Ernie Godfrey, assistant line coach.

"That was an outstanding coaching staff at Ohio State. Look how young Woody (middle, standing) looks. And how about that guy Schembechler (kneeling, second from left)?"

THE OHIO STATE UNIVERSITY
AREA OF STUDENT RELATIONS
INTERCOLLEGIATE ATHLETICS
ST. JOHN ARENA
410 WEST WOODRUFF
COLUMBUS, OHIO 43210

Office of Director

AREA CODE 614
TELEPHONE: 293-2341

Dear Bo,

If you were going to have a sick spell why didn't you have it at our game, for your team didn't look the same without you? On television it appeared that they stuck in there real well but they lacked the coordination that they had against us.

Anne is always accusing me of practicing medicine without...

Woody and I didn't talk often. However, following my heart attack on the eve of the 1970 Rose Bowl game, Woody sent a letter of encouragement.

He asked, "If you were going to have a sick spell why didn't you have it at our game, for your team didn't look the same without you? On television it appeared that they stuck in there real well but they lacked the coordination that they had against us."

He closed saying, "I'll see you next November 21st."

Your old coach,
Woody

CAPTURED IN TIME

Let me tell you something. The day this stops being a meaningful experience for the guys who play is the day we ought to throw the whole damn thing out.

— Bo Schembechler

ometimes it takes just one game. Sometimes it takes a whole season.

There's a point, though, in every great program where something jumps up and tells everybody in the United States of America — hey, we've got something special here.

For me, it was our 1969 victory over Ohio State. That one game made my program. Now we move along to the present and we've got the 1997 team.

In case somebody has been living under a rock and hasn't noticed, Lloyd Carr and his players have made one helluva statement.

Michigan Football is back where it's supposed to be — right on TOP!

There's no other sport like college football where games played 20, 30, or even 50 years ago are just as alive today as they were back then.

We remember key plays. We know what the weather was like. We're able to throw ourselves back in time and feel all of the things that were going on around us.

That's the beauty of college football. As long as there are people around who were there when the game was played, the memories live forever. At a place like Michigan with its long tradition, even some of those games that are 60 and 70 years old keep on getting replayed like one of those old classic movies.

In my career, I was fortunate to have been part of some mighty big ones. Rose Bowls...Ohio State games...Michigan State games.

If I had to pick one, though, none was more important than that 24-12 whipping we put on Ohio State in my first season in 1969.

"Anthony Thomas doesn't only carry the ball, he carries a legacy."

"Every catch seems to be just a little bit better against Ohio State. Just ask Mercury Hayes."

"No one shredded the Ohio State defense like Tshimanga Biakabutuka did with 313 yards in 1995."

That one game sent a message to the whole country. From that day forward, Michigan was back where it was supposed to be.

We were going to be a force to be reckoned with from here on out!

After Woody Hayes retired, I was invited to speak at a banquet in his honor. Security was tight. The only people allowed into the hall were his former players and any assistant who ever coached for him.

I was still coaching at Michigan and I was selected to speak on behalf of all the former assistants.

Some people may have had a little trouble understanding Woody. But I loved the man. He was honest. He was totally dedicated to his beliefs and his team. He was a man of high integrity. And he knew more about football than most coaches in the country put together.

I got up and spoke my piece. When I was finished, Woody walked up to the podium. Before he started, he spotted Dick Brubaker — one of his old players — all the way in the back of the room smoking a cigarette.

"Brubaker," he barked. "Put the damn cigarette out before I start. Now I'm not going to talk if anybody out there is smoking."

Every cigar and cigarette in the place went out. It didn't matter how long ago any of those guys had played for him. No former players were going to smoke when the old coach was speaking.

"That's giving a little extra against Ohio State."

"We had so many great teams here," Woody began. "We had national championships. We have so much to be proud of. But that 1969 squad was probably the most talented football team I ever had. It was a marvelous team."

He proceeded to rattle off a list of names like Rex Kern, Jim Otis, John Brockington, Jack Tatum, and a whole lot more. Then he stopped. He looked down at the end of the table where I was sitting.

"Damn you, Bo," he growled. "You will never win a bigger game than that one!"

Every person in the place roared. We all knew he was right. That one game was the catalyst for everything that came after it at Michigan.

Almost every football expert in every part of the United States of America agreed that the 1969 Ohio State squad was the greatest college team ever assembled.

They were undefeated and national champions in 1968. They were 8-0 and rated No. 1 when they came into Ann Arbor that day. Nobody but my players, my coaches, me, and God thought we even had a chance to stay within two touchdowns of those guys.

But we did it. We did it because we had made a commitment way back around Christmas when I got to Ann Arbor that we were going to beat those guys and put Michigan back where it belongs.

The previous year in Columbus, Woody stuck a knife into Michigan. That wound did not heal till 12 months later when we knocked them off their No. 1 perch. Late in that 1968 game, he went for a two-point conversion after a touchdown to make the score 50-14.

Well, no one at Michigan ever forgot that. I made damn sure none of my players forgot.

Every day starting in spring practice, we did something special to prepare for that game.

The Saturday before that game we went up to Iowa and crushed them, 51-6. And Iowa had a pretty decent team.

After that game before the team even went into the locker room, all the guys gathered in this meeting room. They kept shouting: "Beat Ohio...Beat Ohio...Beat Ohio." They were pounding on each other's shoulders. They were slapping helmets. I mean, man, they were physical.

One of my coaches said, "Bo, they're going to get too high."

I said, "Leave them alone. We will NEVER be too high for this game. Let 'em go."

That whole week before the Ohio State game, I had every one of my demonstration team players wear No. 50 for practice.

"Brian Griese stepped up and became a true 'Michigan Man' in 1997.

It was a wild week. First it snowed. Then we got sleet. The field was unplayable so I had all the freshmen and other guys out there with brooms and shovels so we could practice. The practices were good and crisp, but the weather was terrible.

It was frigid that Friday night before the game. The furnace blew out in the hotel where we were staying. At 2 o'clock in the morning, I got up and rounded up a bunch of blankets. We went around to all the players' rooms and gave them extra blankets.

Everything that could go wrong that week did go wrong. Except for one thing. None of my boys forgot what had happened the previous year.

We took a 24-12 lead into halftime and that same frenzy happened all over again. Jim

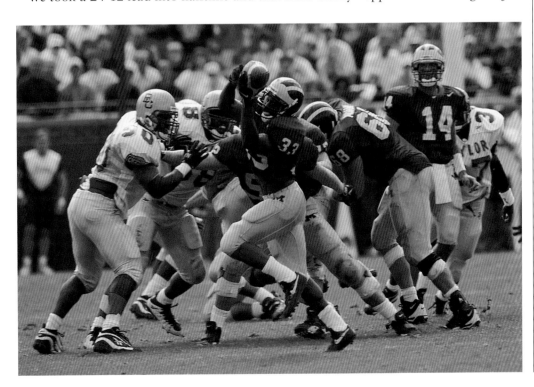

199

Young was one of my coaches. He was very smart but not a very demonstrative sort of person.

He jumped up and yelled: "They will NOT score in the second half! THEY WILL NOT SCORE!"

And, by God, they didn't.

We were ranked 12th going into that game and pulled off one of the biggest upsets in history. Nobody was supposed to beat Ohio State. Not even the great Green Bay Packers.

Well, we did. And Michigan wasn't a 'Nobody' any more.

By the time I got home that night, I was getting phone calls from the media all over the country. It exploded. From that day forward, everybody knew Michigan was back. And you better get ready to deal with us.

Now during the last few seasons, Michigan never failed to win at least eight games. But four losses a year simply doesn't get it, according to Michigan standards.

Lloyd Carr was placed into an awfully awkward position. He took over the team under very difficult circumstances. Even when he was put in charge before the 1995 season, he was termed the "interim coach."

That's tough at any school. At Michigan, it's working with handcuffs.

When you're an interim, how do you go about recruiting the right kids to perform on a national level? How do you go about putting together the right coaching staff?

Well, he did it. He did it quietly. He did it meticulously. And he did it with integrity.

Lloyd Carr recruited tirelessly. He coached each player as if each one were his son. And he set a good example for each one to follow. He put all the pieces together and created his own program that perfectly reflects the Michigan tradition.

There was no single game that established Lloyd as becoming one of the finest coaches in the Michigan tradition. Instead, it was that whole 1997 season when Michigan marched – I mean MARCHED – undefeated through one of the toughest schedules in the country.

Right from the start, there wasn't a Michigan fan on the planet that couldn't sense something special was happening.

It started with Colorado. In some pre-season polls, Colorado was picked to win a national title. When Michigan dominated every single part of that game, everyone could feel – MICH-i-gan is back!

Then it was Notre Dame. Then Michigan State. Then Penn State. And finally Ohio State. One by one, Michigan steam rolled them all.

You must remember that 1997 team didn't just happen. It was three years in the making. And that whole season made a statement that Lloyd Carr is the right man for Michigan and Michigan is right back where it's supposed to be.

"The backwards hat symbolizes another Michigan victory. The band members are used to that."

Since that season Michigan teams have earned the right to play in a major bowl game on New Year's Day every year. Each player – from the most highly touted recruit to the walk-on who has the guts to endure the grind of a season without the glory of the spotlight – has matured into a man and learned to play the game the way it's supposed to be played…the MICH-i-gan way!

As the years go by, each one of those games and each one of those seasons grow a little richer in our memories.

That's what makes college football so great. That's what makes the Michigan Football tradition so special. It's alive. And it keeps on growing.

The best is always yet to come!

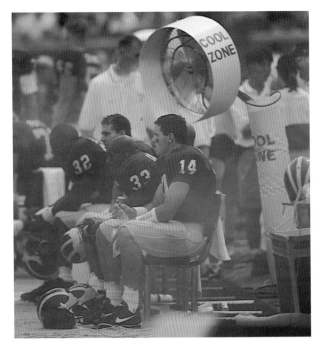

LAST BOWL BEFORE BO

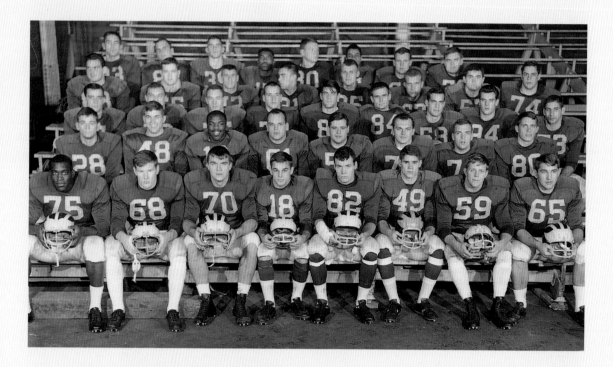

Until Bo turned Michigan into a perennial postseason participant, the Wolverines' lone bowl appearance between 1951 and 1970 came in the 1965 Rose Bowl.

Michigan made the most of that opportunity by squashing Oregon State, 34-7.

For those young men growing up during the turbulent political decade of the '60s, the experience left lifetime memories. Jim Conley captained that team. And he's proud of it for more than just its on-field success.

"In those days, only 44 players were allowed to dress for the Rose Bowl," said Conley. "All but two graduated from Michigan."

That's an incredibly high percentage, but that also was an incredibly gifted team. Except for a 21-20 upset to unranked Purdue in the season's fourth game, Michigan was flawless. The Wolverines outscored their opponents, 235-83. They finished 9-1 and ranked 4th nationally.

Conley carries many fond memories from his Michigan career. None, however, remain as warm as Michigan's 10-0 shutout at Ohio State in the game before that Rose Bowl.

"It was so cold," Conley said. "But we were so excited. I actually felt like I was floating in the air above the field watching everything that was going on down there."

Conley must have enjoyed what he saw because he turned in a spectacular performance. He played end on both sides of the ball and wound up with 12 tackles and 13 assists. Conley was a friend of Bo Rein who played on that Ohio State team.

"He said that Woody Hayes told his guys after the game, 'How could you let that skinny S.O.B. Conley beat you?'" Conley laughed.

Although always competitive, the Michigan teams during that period were not as dominant as after Bo's arrival. Conley played under Bump Elliott, who had been an outstanding player and became a very solid coach. Through the years, Conley has gotten to know Bo well.

"Bo did more for college football than any other one man," Conley said.

"They used to take just 44 players to the Rose Bowl. Bo argued that if they can take 250 members from the band and 300 faculty members then he should be able to take his whole squad. He said he wouldn't go if he couldn't. Bo also was largely responsible for getting the Big Ten to allow its members to play in more games than just the Rose Bowl."

Even more significant to Conley is the manner in which Bo conducted the program.

"Everything was by the book," Conley said. "There was never anything done under the table. Everything was done up front and no individual was bigger than the team.

"Bo symbolizes the Michigan tradition. It's about the team. It's about winning and graduating. He could be a poster boy for what college athletics should be."

Those were some of the precise reasons why Conley chose Michigan over Penn State, Notre Dame, and Dartmouth after graduating from Springdale (PA) High School in 1961.

"There is no other place like the University of Michigan," he said. "You get to meet those who went before you. Guys like Ron Kramer. And you meet those who come afterward. It may sound corny but it really is a big family."

As a sophomore in 1962, Conley and his teammates had the privilege of listening to the legendary Fritz Crisler deliver a speech to them the Friday night before the Ohio State game.

"He was such a powerful speaker," Conley said. "It was moving. I thought some guys were going to cry."

Maybe the speech had some impact because Michigan took Ohio State to a scoreless tie at the half before the Buckeyes ground out a 28-0 victory.

"Imagine what we might have done if Mr. Crisler had spoken at breakfast," Conley cracked.

Nevertheless, it was then that the team made a promise to get back to the Rose Bowl soon. Two years later that promise was kept.

"When I sat in the stands as a freshman, I saw how much Michigan football means to so many people," Conley said. "There are a lot of good football programs around the country. There are a lot of good academic schools. But how many combine those two elements as well as Michigan? None."

Conley is a successful manufacturer's representative for the automobile industry in Dearborn. He still resides in Ann Arbor and remains as rabid a fan as he was a player. Occasionally he's asked to address the team.

That's an easy job for the old captain. That passion for Michigan is one that simply doesn't die.

ATTITUDE MEANS VICTORY

There is no more important job for the head coach than to create a winning attitude.

His primary responsibility is to make sure that every member of the organization maintains the same positive attitude and desire to win. That applies to all the players, all the assistant coaches and all the people who work in the department.

Each coach has his own way of developing attitude. But it must be done before success is realized.

That's a 24-hour a day, seven-day a week job. The head coach must create that attitude and he better work on it on a daily basis.

It's very easy to see in a football player someone who is not performing up to expectations. The head coach must find out why that is happening and he must address the problem immediately!

I've always felt that when a problem exists in an individual player or with a team, you must attack that problem now. You do not take the problem home. You do not sleep on it. You attack. If you have attacked it incorrectly, you can always apologize. But if you let that problem sit, you can not have a good, tough, disciplined football program. That's impossible.

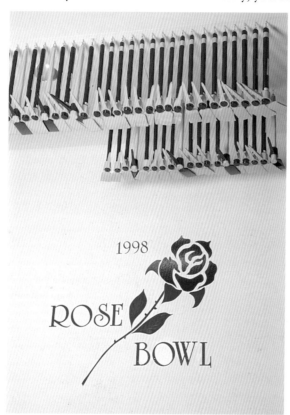

1998 ROSE BOWL

Without attitude, there is no victory!

You can not develop that attitude on game day. You can not do it simply in a pre-game meeting with a "win one for the Gipper" speech. That can help. But that alone won't get the job done. Attitude must be built at the beginning of the year. Then it must be maintained daily throughout the season.

Everyone saw what Lloyd Carr did with the 1997 team. That was the result of attitude. And it didn't just happen overnight.

As long as I coached and even today in retirement, the first thing I look for is when the team comes out of that tunnel. Right then I can tell if the team is ready to play that day. More than anything else, that is the responsibility of the head coach.

Attitude is a daily job. And how well you perform that job determines how well the team will finish.

"Coach Carr inspired his 1997 team that each play of each game must be executed one step at a time, just like climbing that impossible mountain. Each player received a pick that hung in the team meeting room thoughout the season. Once they made it to the top, each one received his pick symbolic of that long climb to the National Championship."

"Champions must set goals and then stick to them."

"We certainly know how to draw a crowd."

"The Cadets have arrived. And Michigan is going to march them right out."

THE TOUCHDOWN THAT NEVER WAS

"It was a fumble then...and it's still a fumble now."

That's the way Bo and most of the rest of a disbelieving national television audience saw the play on which Charles White scored a phantom touchdown in Southern California's 17-10 victory over Michigan in the 1979 Rose Bowl.

"It was so obvious," Bo still maintains today. "It wasn't even close. White was hit before he crossed the plane (of the goal line) and fumbled the ball on the three-yard line."

The controversial play occurred in the second quarter with USC leading, 7-3.

"If that call had been made properly, we had a chance to win," Bo said. "Stopping that drive and recovering the fumble put momentum on our side."

To this day, Bo understands perhaps why the line judge first made the call. But he still does not understand why the other officials did not overrule the decision.

"There might have been players on his (line judge) side of the field that hid his view," Bo said. "When White dived, the official assumed he had the ball. Well, the ball was back on the three-yard line where Jerry Meter recovered it."

The umpire, in fact, signaled first down for Michigan. But he was overruled by the official who first made the call.

"It was the worst call I'd ever seen," Bo said.

Long after the game, Bo commiserated with his coaches in his hotel room. The sports news was on television and White was being interviewed.

"The funny thing was when White was explaining he had scored a touchdown, the reporters had a record of Frank Sinatra's song 'It's Impossible' playing in the background," Bo said.

A few years later, Bo ran into White at a Heisman Trophy banquet.

"I walked up to him and said, 'White you fumbled that ball,'" Bo said. "He looked at me and smiled and said, 'ah...well,'"

It was the touchdown that never happened. As Bo says...it was a fumble then and is still a fumble now.

"That's the 1979 Rose Bowl and that's still a fumble by USC's Charles White!"

"At least one official got it right."

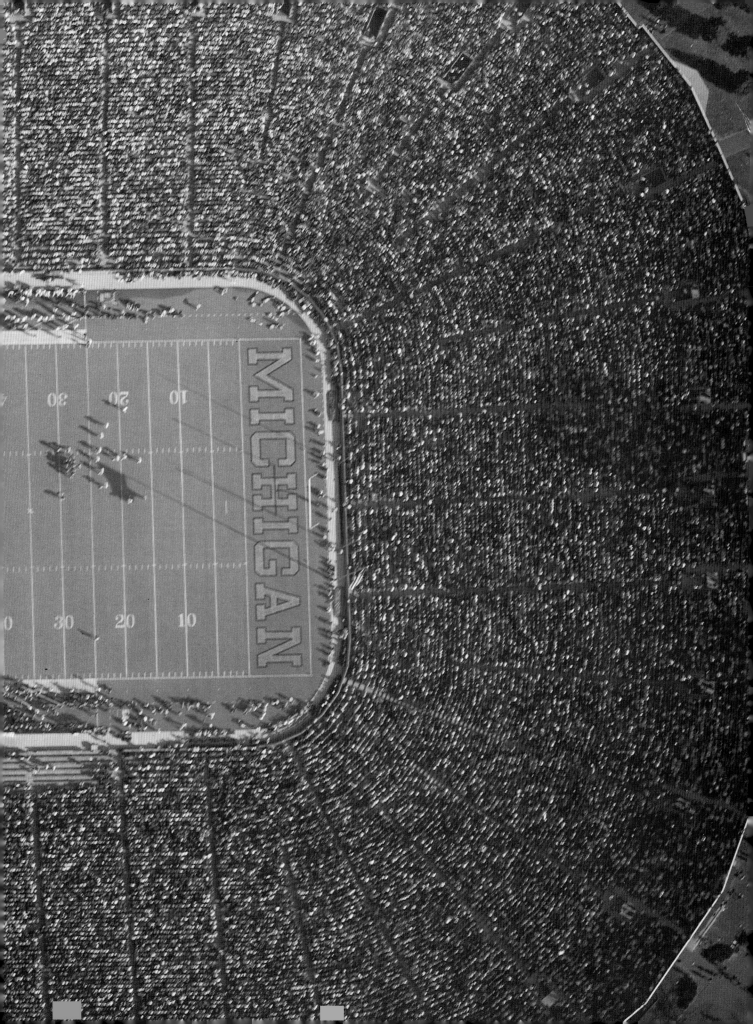

THE TIMES THEY ARE A CHANGIN'

There are problems in the game today...We must try to make them right and uphold the great tradition that this game has established. — **Bo Schembechler**

No sport carries the color...the spectacle...the tra-DI-tion of college football. There's just something special about the game. It creates a feeling that's impossible to explain.

That's why I'm concerned with the direction it's headed.

Over the last few years, the changes in college football have been enormous. I don't know if there's more interest now, but there's a whole lot more emphasis on the game from the way it's treated in the media.

There's investigative reporting. There are certain negative writers who go out of their way to nitpick about some things they know absolutely nothing about. The only purpose of some radio talk shows seems to see which host can scream the loudest. And there are some TV sports shows that make about as much sense as adding more games to the schedule. All these things bring more pressure to the game.

There are more demands on coaches. More demands on players. Ticket prices have gone up and stadiums have been expanded.

Without a doubt, though, the biggest change is the amount of money that's involved. And doesn't trouble always find a way to follow money?

In my mind, all these things have detracted from the most important reason to play the game. That's scholastics and participation by the student-athletes.

I get a kick out of some college presidents and conference commissioners. They talk about increasing academic standards and making sure everything is right for the student-athletes. But when a network comes in and lays the money on the line, they really don't give a damn what it means to the player. They take the money and run.

The NCAA has conducted all kinds of studies to determine what is best for the student-athletes. But the truth of the matter is when networks lay the money on the table, college presidents and conference commissioners do whatever they're asked to do. They forget about the great tradition of the game. They forget about what's best for the student-athletes.

They're focused on one thing – money. So what do they do? They create what is called a national championship and make as much money as they can.

College football today is run by the networks to the tune of money. And I think it's gone way too far.

Why are we so obsessed with a national championship? It really doesn't determine the best team in the country. And it detracts significantly from what the game is truly about.

What about tradition? What about the importance of competing for a conference championship? What about maintaining the tremendous rivalries between certain schools and certain conferences that are the very foundation of college football tradition?

In my opinion, the BCS is a complete failure. And all we hear about, even before the season kicks off, is what teams are expected to compete for the national championship.

Who cares?

It's impossible to have a true national champion when all teams don't play each other. It's diluted the very essence of the game. And if you water down tradition long enough, eventually that tradition becomes eroded.

Who cares about the rankings? What difference does it make if one poll rates a certain school over another? People can argue about it during the whole off-season. That's a tradition itself.

We've done the same thing with so many individual awards. Besides the Heisman Trophy, we now have awards for the best receiver, the best lineman, the best running back, the best quarterback, the best linebacker and on and on and on. There's probably even an award for the best water boy.

What does it all mean? It's all individual stuff. The team becomes secondary and that's NOT RIGHT!

In 1985, we started the year with a defense that had not one preseason All-American or All Big Ten selection. No highly touted individual at all. By the middle of the season we had one of the finest defenses in the country and the writers didn't know how to explain it because there had been no individual preseason hype.

I think it's gone way too far. We don't know what's going to happen when players think they are being used to generate revenue to run the vast programs that have been created today.

When I started, we played nine games a year. That didn't generate enough money so then we went to 10. Then 11. Now it's 12 games a year. For conferences with championship games it's 13. Add on a postseason bowl and some teams are playing 14 games.

When does it end?

Players have to train all year long. If they don't work out in the summer, they are not going to play in the fall.

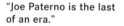

"Joe Paterno is the last of an era."

"Lloyd Carr demands character as much as talent from his recruits."

It's the same thing for coaches. The days of Woody Hayes and Bear Bryant and Tom Osborne and Joe Paterno and Lavell Edwards are gone. The 20-year coach at one university is history because the pressure on him is too great. Even if they are successful, they may not want to go 20 years.

It's too difficult. It takes too much of a toll. There are some within a coach's own school who believe there's too much emphasis on football and they start to grumble. If a coach doesn't have to do it to live, he better have a tremendous love for the game.

It all gets down to one simple thing – college presidents must stand up and say enough is enough!

Football is asked to underwrite the budgets for the entire athletic programs at the major schools. And then they went out and cut football scholarships to 85.

That's just NOT RIGHT and I'll show you why!

When I came to Michigan, I had 105 grant-in-aids. It allowed us to practice HARD. It allowed us to learn all the basic techniques of blocking and tackling without fear of losing players to injury.

When you're limited to 85 scholarships, the truth of the matter is that you're actually working with 60 players because about 25 are freshmen.

You must understand that when you recruit players, one will be just what you expected. Another will contribute to the program, but won't necessarily be good enough to start. The third guy – and I don't care how good an evaluator you are – is going to be a mistake. Out of that 60, now you're down to 40 good players.

When you go to practice, there will be at least 10 who will be temporarily injured and unable to participate. Now you're down to 30 with 11 on offense and 11 on defense with a few guys on special teams. So when the first guy goes down, you're in trouble.

That's why there are so many injuries in football today. They can't develop that toughness in practice. A little bump and they get a serious injury. That's why you lose so many of them.

"Fewer scholarships lead to a lot more injuries."

They can't take as many hits in practice today as when I coached. In areas where you should be able to protect yourself and learn how to tackle properly, you can't practice because someone might get hurt.

The demands on the player today are so great. They do more weight training and conditioning to compensate for not being able to practice the way they should because they don't have enough players.

The solution is simple. Add 15 grants and make freshmen ineligible. The purpose of the freshmen is to help on the demonstration team during the week and learn the fundamentals and techniques of your program.

Don't allow freshmen to face the pressure of going out there to play in front of 110,000 people even before they take one step into a classroom. First, let them get acclimated to going to college. Next, have them work on football fundamentals in order to compete in spring practice for the opportunity to play as a sophomore.

When you follow this program, you are helping these young men with the one thing all these college presidents talk about – academics. That first year, each young man works on academics and getting himself established. Now isn't that a simple solution?

Now the antifootball factions will argue this is only taking care of the men in one program.

Let me ask one simple question – who pays the bills?

Football…and for the entire athletic department!

What must happen, in order to be fair, is to devise a plan that makes sense for everyone. The purpose of college sports is participation. Now how can we encourage participation without breaking the back of football?

One solution is to not issue scholarships to every person who plays a sport. If a university has 25 varsity sports and decides it wants to compete nationally in each one, you are going to kill football. It's impossible to generate that kind of revenue.

Wouldn't it be wiser to select three or four men sports and three or four women sports and finance them to the maximum in order to compete on a national scale? The rest of the sports would compete in the conference and on a more local basis.

To me, that seems like common sense.

There's no question that because of the huge amounts of money involved and the enormous amount of media coverage that college football generates, there are problems in the game today that no one could have imagined even 10 years ago.

That's why it is so critical today for a major university to have a coach who is honest...is dedicated to his program and isn't looking over his shoulder to jump at another job for a little more money...and can instill those same qualities into the players he recruits to his school.

We are very fortunate to have Lloyd Carr here at Michigan. When I recruited, I looked as much for character in a young man as I did for talent. That's the same thing Lloyd does. A young man can have all the talent in the world, but if he lacks character he's only half a player.

There are problems in the game today. Big problems. We must try to make them right and uphold the great tradition that this game has established.

"No one can change this tradition."

A TIME FOR THANKS

Success in the future is based upon success of the past.

— Bo Schembechler

Walking off the field after we beat Ohio State in 1989, I pretty much knew it would be my last trip through that tunnel.

I didn't give it much thought at the time. We had just beaten Ohio State, 28-18. Any game with that team is a killer for both sides. And we had to start preparing for the Rose Bowl.

But I sort of knew.

Looking back, it's easier to put things into perspective. And the bottom line is how amazingly powerful Michigan Football really is.

Fielding H. Yost once coached here. Then he was gone.

Fritz Crisler coached here. So did Bennie Oosterbaan and Bump Elliott.

All of them were marvelous. All of them made tremendous contributions. But no single man is responsible for the overall excellence of the Michigan tradition.

In academics or athletics, the true test of excellence is time. No other yardstick is a greater measure.

Success in the classroom or on the football field often is discovered by the good ones. The great ones, however, are able to do it year after year after year.

That's the mark of a champion. And for more than a century now, that's the standard which the University of Michigan has set.

That is the heart and soul of tradition. And it's as alive today as it was before Fielding H. Yost even came up with the idea to dig that big hole in the ground and build the most magnificent stadium in college football anywhere in the country.

It's been 35 years now since I was first given the privilege of becoming part of this great tradition. There were many great moments. There were a few I'd like to forget.

But I wouldn't trade one second for having had the opportunity to become at least one small part of the greatest university in the world.

We won championships. We won bowl games. Hopefully we created memories which every Michigan graduate and fan will cherish for a lifetime.

More importantly than all of that, we accomplished all those things by doing it the Michigan way. We did it with honesty and integrity.

Today, I get no bigger thrill than going out

Cathy never saw me coach or she probably never would have married me.

to that stadium on a fall Saturday afternoon. I sit up in the press box now. Before the game starts, I look around at all those people packed into those stands. I appreciate how much that football team means to all of them.

And when I watch those young men come charging out of that tunnel, I still get the same chills as I did when I ran out of there for all those years.

Each game is a battle because each game is for Michigan. I can feel all those goose bumps that the players and the coaches and the trainers and everyone on the field gets. And I know — win or lose — those young men are going to fight for MICH-i-gan. They won't leave that field till every drop of sweat is gone.

Coach Lloyd Carr appreciates the significance of the Michigan tradition. He honors it. He understands that success in the future is based on the success of the past. No one person is bigger than the University.

That's exactly why his football teams will continue to excel. They'll succeed under the same Michigan standards that were established long before he or I arrived in Ann Arbor. They'll succeed because of hard work...dedication...honesty...and integrity.

Somewhere down the road, Coach Carr will be gone. Another coach will receive the privilege of becoming part of the finest football program in the country.

The University of Michigan is about excellence. And it's filled with tra-DI-tion!

PHOTO CREDITS

Joseph Arcure: i, iii, viii, ix, x, 4, 6(both), 7(top), 9(both), 10(both), 11, 12,(both), 13, 14(both), 15(top), 16(top and center), 17(both), 18, 19, 20, 21, 24, 25(all), 27(bottom), 29(both), 30, 31(both), 32(both), 33, 35(bottom), 37(both), 39(bottom), 41(bottom), 42, 44(top right and bottom left), 45(bottom), 46(bottom), 47(both), 48(bottom), 55(bottom right), 56(all), 57, 58, 59, 61, 62(both), 63, 64(top), 70,71, 72, 75(both), 76, 77, 78(top), 79, 80, 82(top), 83(both), 84(bottom), 87(top), 89, 90(both), 91, 92, 93, 94, 97, 101(bottom), 102(all), 104(both), 106(both), 107, 108, 109(both), 110, 111(all), 112(both), 113(all), 114-5, 116, 120(bottom), 127(bottom), 130(top), 139, 144, 145, 146, 147, 149, 150, 161, 164, 169, 170(both), 171(both), 180(both), 181(top), 182(bottom), 183, 184(both), 185(both), 186(top), 189, 194, 195, 196(both), 197, 198, 199(both), 200, 201(both), 202(both), 203(both), 205, 206, 207(both), 208(bottom), 214

Allsport USA: 106(bottom), 200

Ann Arbor News: 22, 23, 28 (top right and left), 43(top), 44(top left and bottom right), 45(top), 48(top), 49(both), 50(both), 96(bottom), 99, 105(top right), 140, 141, 142

AP/Wide World Photos: 81(bottom), 95(top), 157, 186(bottom), 209

Carolyn Arcure: 148

Bentley Historical Library: 3, 7(bottom), 15(bottom), 16(bottom), 27 (top), 34(both), 35(top), 38(bottom), 40, 41(top), 40, 43(bottom), 46(top), 51, 52(both), 53, 54(both), 55(bottom left), 60(bottom), 64(bottom), 65(bottom), 66(top), 68, 69, 73, 82(bottom), 84(top), 85, 87(bottom), 100, 117, 118, 119, 121, 122, 123(both), 124(bottom), 125, 126(both), 127(top), 128, 131, 132, 136, 137, 138, 143, 159, 160(bottom), 172, 174, 176, 177, 178, 181(bottom), 182(top), 187, 191(both)

Don Canham: 26

The Dufek Family: 81(top)

Gerald Ford: vii

Mike Gittleson: 151, 152, 153

The Harbaugh Family: 78(bottom)

Bob Kalmbach: 10(top), 65(top), 66(bottom), 166, 167, 168, 173(both), 208(top),

Photair, Inc.: 212-3

Bo Schembechler: 89, 98, 156, 165, 175, 192, 193, 210, 211, 221

Sports Illustrated: 91, 106(top)

Pete Stanger: 5, 8, 55(top), 86, 88, 95(bottom), 96(top), 120(top), 129, 130(bottom), 158

David Ufer: 103, 133

University of Michigan Athletic Media Relations: 74, 105(top left and bottom)

OTHER GREAT MICHIGAN TITLES FROM HURON RIVER PRESS
Publishing Great Books of the Great Lakes

Voelker's Pond: A Robert Traver Legacy

Some knew him as University of Michigan alumni and Michigan Supreme Court judge John Voelker, some knew him as best-selling writer Robert Traver who wrote *Anatomy of a Murder*. Still others, like Charles Kuralt, called him "the closest thing to a great man [he] ever met." Stunning photography and reminiscences share with you the man, his one-roomed cabin, and the glacial pond where brook trout remain elusive.

The Common Grill Cookbook

Take a journey of exquisite flavor! Chef Craig Common offers secrets to 161 of his well-loved recipes, including Firecracker Shrimp with Hong Kong Salsa, Seafood Chowder, and Sautéed Walleye with Citrus Butter. The Common Grill Restaurant is located in Chelsea, Michigan.

The Great Lakes Cottage Book

For centuries, people have been drawn to the edges of the Great Lakes in order to build magical places that they can escape to for weekends and vacations. Through essays and photographs Ed and Kathy-jo Wargin capture some of these retreats.

Views from the Sleeping Bear: Photographs of the Sleeping Bear Dunes National Lakeshore

Explore the dunes of Lake Michigan in *Views from the Sleeping Bear*. Celebrating Michigan's greatest gift of nature, accomplished writer and photographer Thomas Kachadurian captures the magnificence of Lake Michigan's shores, where visitors have been drawn for over a century.

Vintage Views of Leelanau County

Take an incredible look back in time at Leelanau County, known as the "Land of Delight." Authors M. Christine Byron and Thomas R. Wilson share images from their collection of 1,400 postcards compiled over the past 15 years.

Corporate and volume sales are available for all titles. Please call 1-800-956-8999. Huron River Press, 320 N. Main Street, Chelsea, MI 48118.

Books on golf - http://www.clocktowerpress.com
Books on Michigan - http://www.huronriverpress.com